HOW
WRITING
WORKS

Learning and Using
the Processes

HOW WRITING WORKS

Learning and Using the Processes

FRANCIS A. HUBBARD
Marquette University

ST. MARTIN'S PRESS   New York

Senior Editor: Nancy Perry
Development Editor: Michael Weber
Project Editor: Beverly Hinton
Production Supervisor: Julie Toth
Cover Design: Judy Forster

For information, write:
St. Martin's Press, Inc.
175 Fifth Avenue
New York, NY 10010

ISBN: 0-312-89467-8

For Ben

To the Instructor

How Writing Works was written to answer as many "hows" and "whys" as possible. When an instructor announces some obvious truth about writing, such as that an essay has a beginning, a middle, and an end, it is the brighter student who asks, "Why?" And it is the active learner who asks, of the answer the instructor provides, yet *another* "why." Why should sentences vary in length? Because readers would get bored. But how and why would sentences of similar length bore a reader, rather than make the material easier to assimilate?

When writing instructors can answer several such questions in a row, I believe we have begun to do our job. When we have encouraged students to ask several such questions in a row, we have gotten them to begin to do theirs. All the more reason, then, for our textbooks and courses to avoid arbitrary pronouncements and instead to encourage inquiry. Why are examples effective? Why use concrete details? Why are paragraphs necessary? Through such questions we make progress toward a better understanding of "how writing works."

I have offered answers to such questions by looking at what readers do as they read, well aware that these answers lead to additional questions, perhaps more interesting ones still. I have left room for experienced teachers to supplement the text with further answers. But at the same time I have made the writing activities in the text rich enough in themselves so that beginning teachers can rely on their students to find many useful answers. Most of all, however, I have encouraged the inquiry process itself, believing that experienced and inexperienced teachers alike would prefer that atmosphere in their classes.

Perhaps the most difficult "why" for instructors to answer is "why should I write this assignment?" I believe beginning writers—freshmen are generally beginners in the sense that they have not experienced much of what writing can do—first need points about writing from which to take off. So my answer to that fundamental "why?" is that the assignments allow students to experience what writing will be like for *them*. The very first assignment, which merely requires students to paraphrase, is meant to begin providing the experience in question.

How Writing Works is built on a sequence of such assignments or activities. My exposition is meant as accompaniment to the main business of a writing course as I conceive it: students writing, discussing writing, and then writing some more. I have tried to write a book which stays out of the way of this main business, by simply arranging what students do in a useful order and allowing students to discover for themselves the points about writing that they need in order to generate, structure, and present their thoughts. *What the students write is the main text of the course.* I hope in this way to help students continue to improve their writing after they leave the writing course by establishing a pattern of self-guided learning which is also self-sustaining.

A key assumption of my particular kind of writing activity is that language use will improve with awareness. As we speak and write, much of what happens linguistically must be automatic; there isn't time to consider everything. But all the parts of writing, from generating ideas to proofreading, seem to me to benefit from de-automating. I mean the activities in this book to bring attention to the ways we get ideas, the ways we reason, the ways we structure and arrange, the ways we polish and present, and above all the ways writing works for each of us. It is this awareness, I believe, more than anything else we do in writing classes, that will prepare our students for the writing tasks they must perform in the future.

There are enough activities in *How Writing Works* so that an entire course can be built by doing each in turn, however briefly, and I have taught my own course this way. But a better plan, I think, is to allow students to revise some few that they select (say, four) from the set of activities you require (say, twenty) and compile them in a portfolio to be submitted at the end of the course. Better still, perhaps, is to require that students *construct*, out of groups of activities, three or four papers, revised again into a portfolio.

In Chapter One, for example, a paper could be written on the effects of paraphrasing. In the paper, the student would examine the "Star-Spangled Banner," the Pledge of Allegiance, a prayer, a song, and some other piece he or she knows "by heart," comparing the effects of paraphrasing through these five experiences. Has paraphrasing been helpful? How might the automatic character of these pieces be defined? Could the de-automating effect be achieved in other ways? And so on. As I have reused these materials, I have grown comfortable with this last method, although it may not be suitable the first time you use the book.

I have indicated, where I could naturally do so, how essays

may develop out of the activities. Since I did not want to interrupt the exposition with sections that might not be necessary, more on essay development may be found in the instructor's manual.

The activities, of course, do not need to be done *in toto*. Some can be left to students to read and think about. I have tried to include a sufficient number so that no one activity is critical for any chapter (with the exception of the first in Chapter One). Courses on the quarter system may have time for only one activity per chapter, which need not be written out. And even if activities are written out, they may not always need a full-length response. Sometimes a few minutes suffice to articulate the necessary points. This is not true of the information-gathering activities which send students out in all directions and then bring them back to compare what each has found.

To be consistent with my approach to writing, I have written a textbook which *cannot* be followed exactly or step by step. Instead, I have supplied materials and suggested experiences, out of which readers (instructors) can create their own courses from which *their* readers (students) can construct *their* own.

ACKNOWLEDGMENTS

The sequence of assignments on which this book is based was written during the NEH/University of Iowa Institute on Writing in 1979. Credit for getting me to see what I was trying to do belongs to the staff of that Institute: Carl H. Klaus, Richard Lloyd-Jones, David Hamilton, Cleo Martin, Lou Kelly, and visitor William E. Coles, Jr. In particular the research project of Nancy Jones and the chance to write about the sequence in *Courses for Change* (Boynton-Cook, 1984), edited by Carl H. Klaus and Nancy Jones, helped me understand how such a book could be written.

This book has taken several years to write, and a number of very capable people have had a hand in it. Both my oldest and most recent debts are to Karen Pelz of Western Kentucky University, who encouraged me long ago to think I could write it and whose careful and supportive reviews have had much to do with my completing it. Stanley E. Fish, Jr., now of Duke University, taught me much of what I know about reading. Tom Broadbent, then of St. Martin's Press, gave me the impetus to begin, and Nancy Perry of St. Martin's has given me the will to continue; Michael Weber has been a patient and helpful editor as I have finished. In addition I would like to thank my other reviewers, who went out of their way to show me what I was doing that they found useful: David Bartholomae of the University of Pittsburgh, Patricia Burnes of the University of Maine at Orono, Cleo Martin of the University of Iowa, Thomas Newkirk of the University of New Hampshire, Mike Rose of the University of California at Los Angeles, Nancy Sommers of Harvard University, and Ross Winterowd of the University of Southern California.

The people who have made the greatest difference to this book have been the students who have tried it and told me what was wrong. Anonymous students from the class of Laurie Ewert-Krocker at Cleveland State; Cindy Carpenter, Rick Lewis, and Lisa Ward from California State University at Sacramento; and Bob Neura, Charles Park, and Carl Smith from Cleveland State will all recognize that I took their suggestions seriously.

Francis A. Hubbard

Contents

PART TWO
LEARNING TO WRITE FOR READERS 37

PART THREE
RETHINKING WRITING   91

Chapter 6   How Writing Persuades   93

Chapter 7   How People Reason   107

Chapter 8   How People Structure
and Organize   124

Chapter 9   How People Manage Sentences
and Words   133

PART FOUR
IMPROVING YOUR WRITING   151

Chapter 10   The Glamor of Grammar   153

Chapter 11   Style and Voice   168

Chapter 12   Revising and Editing   177

Chapter 13   Learning to Write All Over
Again   189

Index   193

To the Student

As you begin this book, you probably know some reasons for improving your writing. You want to do well in college, and you know you'll have to write essay exams and term papers. You want a good job, and you know you'll have to write good proposals and reports.

These are good reasons for learning how to write better. They are also external reasons, reasons outside you, the learner. These reasons focus on what *other* people will get out of your improved writing: They will see more clearly that you have learned your history, your psychology, your economics; or later on they will get the information they need from your reports. The benefits to you are *indirect*, coming through their approval.

Are there *direct* benefits to you in learning to write better? The answer is "yes," although as Joe Louis once said, "There are some people that, if they don't know, you can't tell 'em." For one thing, the direct benefits are not the same for everyone; different people find that writing does different things for them. In addition, the benefits are almost impossible to understand or believe until you have experienced them, so Louis is right again: Until you know, no one can tell you why writing will be important to you and in what ways.

The most we can do in writing courses and textbooks is to help you find out and experience what writing can do for you. Then, once you discover what you will use writing for, you will learn techniques and strategies much more easily because they won't seem arbitrary. They will connect directly to what you really want to do.

A best-selling book provides an example of what I am talking about. Every year in this country more than five million blank journals and diaries are sold. Many people have discovered, entirely on their own, that keeping a diary or journal lets them watch themselves as they live their lives and gives them the chance to live more fully, regardless of how they actually keep the diary and make entries in it.

People who haven't actually kept a diary wouldn't understand. ("If they don't know . . ."). And people who do keep journals or diaries probably wouldn't give the same reasons why they keep them; published writers seem to have as many uses for them as there are writers. Still, just the simple activity of recording thoughts at regular intervals does provide for many people one of the benefits I was talking about and does give an internal reason for writing.

We know from recent research that people improve their writing more easily and more quickly when they are learning for internal reasons, for their own purposes and for immediate benefits. Since I cannot know what those purposes and benefits are for you, however, I cannot *sell* writing to you. All I can do, all this book tries to do, all your writing course can do, is give you as many of the experiences as possible that other writers have found valuable. Then you can make up your own mind what to pursue and what to leave out.

Research also shows that we learn by doing. It is especially true of writing, apparently, that lots of talk about writing isn't as much help as a little actual doing of it, in situations as realistic as possible. The more isolated a particular writing activity is from the way writing is actually used, the less helpful it seems to be—I am thinking particularly of drills on grammar and usage. Unless you have written the drill yourself (see Chapter Ten, "The Glamor of Grammar"), you will probably retain very little of it.

Many of the writing activities in this book are meant to be like writing done by managers, engineers, lawyers, doctors, technicians, political workers, teachers, and others. Think of the procedure of a working group, in which each person investigates some part of a problem and brings in a brief report, which the group as a whole analyzes, puts together with all the other reports into a larger report, and then implements. Such activities are common in this book because they make it possible for you to learn from twenty or more people instead of merely from one, as well as because they are like the writing you can expect to do after college. They have the added advantage that everyone's contribution counts, rather than being just repetitious busywork.

Since writers are so different and since writing situations vary so much, I don't present a method which you *have* to follow. Instead, I have built each chapter around several activities from which you can get material to write about, and I have made suggestions about how to do that writing. I hope your experiences with these activities will help you design flexible writing processes to meet your needs both during college and after, processes that suit your personality as a writer as well as the readers you will encounter. I hope they will let you find out how writing works for you and encourage you to continue to develop as a writer after the course is over.

The best approach for you, I think, is experimental. Students who have worked with these activities have not done identical work. Each one has done something different, and the student writers who have tried new things wholeheartedly, who have gone to extremes, and who have extended their own methods, approaches, and structures beyond what they started with have often told me afterward that they weren't sure they got what I intended, but they had gotten something useful. *That was in fact all I intended.*

HOW WRITING WORKS

Learning and Using the Processes

PART ONE

LEARNING AND READING

While you work with these first two chapters, you will focus on *learning* and *reading*. The activities ask you to examine a successful learning experience of your own and to explain—among other things—what kind of reader you are. These activities are meant to help you understand how to become a better writer. You can also use them as the basis for a paper, or at least the draft of a paper (revising is discussed in later chapters), about you as a learner. As you work through these two chapters, consider the activities as providing occasions to draft sections of this larger paper, which you can then fit together into a whole.

CHAPTER 1

How People Learn

THE POINT OF THIS CHAPTER

The beginnings of books and chapters are for setting goals. In this chapter, we will look closely at learning. Your experiences with the activities in this chapter should remind you of how you learn best and help you use that successful way of learning to improve your writing.

You probably don't learn things exactly the way anyone else does. Perhaps this fact bothers you when you see how easily someone else can learn from a lecture or realize that someone is learning a subject that you have worked hard to master just by discussing it with you.

But perhaps you can also remember a time when you grasped something almost at first sight while others were having difficulty. If you are like most people, you probably like to learn certain kinds of things; that is part of the reason that you can sometimes learn at first sight. But *how* you learn is also important, and that is the part of learning that you almost always can control. It therefore makes sense to examine your favorite methods at the beginning of this writing course.

Some people learn easily and quickly from lectures; others learn easily and quickly only from discussion with others. There are

3

many other variables in people's learning, as well. This chapter will allow you to examine closely the ways in which *you* learn most easily and naturally so that you can use them to improve your writing. Because no writing course can fit everyone perfectly, this chapter is designed to help you adapt to the writing course you are taking.

In the first two activities, you will examine some learning you have already done. In the third activity, you will see how others learn, so that you will have some useful alternatives to guide you in developing your learning methods. We will then consider some of the implications of these activities, especially in relation to the nature of learning. Finally, we will look at ways you can learn to improve your writing.

ACTIVITY 1–1: PARAPHRASING

In a career more than twenty years long, a baseball player such as Willie Mays or Reggie Jackson or Don Baylor probably listened to the "Star-Spangled Banner" more than 4,000 times. If each rendition took two minutes, then these players spent more than 8,000 minutes listening to the National Anthem—more than sixteen workdays of eight hours each, more than three workweeks for most of us.

You may not have spent three weeks of your life listening to the National Anthem, but you probably know it pretty well. Write out the words of the first verse. Make notes of where you had difficulties.

Now write a paraphrase of the Anthem, putting it into your own words. Try to rephrase everything so that none of the original is left except its meaning. Again make notes of where you had difficulties.

Many of the activities in this book can form the basis of essays. An essay is literally a "try," an attempt to explore something. You can think of an essay also as a "thought experiment," a lab report on ideas or thoughts or arguments that you have tested against experience or other data. Like other lab reports, an essay does not always say everything about how the experiment went, because audiences are generally more interested in the results. But there is often room for a "methods" section in which an essay writer explains *how* results were reached, in addition to sections on results and significance.

Also like lab reports, essays may fit a strictly controlled format or have variations of their own, depending on the criteria established by those who will read them. If these requirements of format are strict, the writer might need to revise several times before meeting them; if not, the writer can concentrate on revising other matters. Revision is discussed more later on, especially in Chapter Twelve. For now, the important aspect of essays is their exploratory character. The next section is exploratory in this way; in it I try to say what I think paraphrasing shows. It is a "try" in the sense that I wrote it by thinking about the connections I see between paraphrasing and learning. It is not yet an essay, because it is meant instead to fit into this chapter, but it could become an essay if necessary.

MEMORIZING AND PARAPHRASING

Paraphrasing is a useful skill for almost any field of study or work. It means "phrasing" or wording something alongside (or *para*) the original. Paraphrases can be shorter or longer than the original, depending on the purpose: Are you paraphrasing a book to summarize for some notes you are taking? Are you paraphrasing an article or chapter to show someone else that you understand? Are you paraphrasing a difficult paragraph to make sure every little detail is unmistakably clear to you as you read?

When you first learned the National Anthem, you probably memorized it. You heard it over and over again, getting a few more of the words each time until you had enough to make it through. Just trying to write it out now, however, may have convinced you that memorization isn't always the best way to learn things. You might have encountered gaps in your memory, misunderstandings, and other problems, such as difficulty remembering what comes next unless you have the music to guide you.

Paraphrasing something you have memorized will almost always show you new meaning in it, which is, of course, virtually a definition of learning. Paraphrasing the "Star-Spangled Banner" helps you learn something more about the Anthem even when you thought you had already learned all there was to it. What causes this?

The key seems to be putting the text of the Anthem into your own words. When you do that, you move it closer to your own experience. By choosing words that you have used elsewhere you connect the Anthem, at least a little bit, to other parts of your life. Your new understanding of the Anthem can even influence your life to a certain extent. For example, on the next Fourth of July, you might see more clearly why we feel such a strong connection between fireworks ("rockets" and "bombs") and our independence. So you move closer to the Anthem as well.

Even more important than the words you choose, however, is the deliberate act of choosing them yourself, because it is something you *do* rather than just something you hear about. Most people would agree that they remember 10 percent of what they hear, 20 percent of what they see—and 90 percent of what they do. It seems to be a general learning principle that the more actively engaged we are with a task, the more we learn from it. The more passive we are and the less we try to make our own sense of things, the less we will retain. So it's not surprising that paraphrasing should help you learn more effectively than memorizing and repeating.

In general, writing works exactly like an extension of paraphrasing. According to many people, good writing is always *effective* writing, or, in other words, it is writing that manages to make a difference, that changes things forever inside the writer and inside the reader. Now, if you sit down to write and tell yourself that your writing must make permanent changes inside you and inside everyone who reads it, you might feel so outmatched that you cannot go ahead. But you won't feel intimidated if you remember that even the act of paraphrasing something as familiar as the National Anthem can permanently rearrange your sense of what the original means. If putting your own words alongside those of the Anthem can change your feelings about it and about a national holiday, then your original writing can surely change a reader. The natural and almost inevitable effect of writing about anything is to help you consider your topic in the same detail and with the same attention you gave to paraphrasing the Anthem. This is one way writing works.

You can benefit from the example of paraphrasing not only in writing, but also in learning to write. If you expect someone to tell you how you should write, you might get some useful advice and you might not. If you try to memorize the advice, you simply delay the tasks of deciding whether the advice is any good and (if it is) of making the advice work for you. As we shall see in Chapter Three, however, writers are so different from each other that good advice for one writer might be terrible advice for another. So memorizing advice might actually be less than helpful; to paraphrase Mark Twain, it isn't ignorance that hurts us so much as the things we "know" that are wrong for us.

Paraphrasing also shows how one person's good advice can be another person's bad advice. Some people naturally want to paraphrase word by word. They have a lot of trouble with "the land of the free and the home of the brave" because these are already fairly familiar words and because it is hard to find equivalent words that don't sound foolish—like "the domicile of the courageous." Where these paraphrasers do their best work, by contrast, is in the parts of the original Anthem that have a definite pattern of words that they want to retain—say, the questions of the first stanza ('. . . can you see . . . ?"), which become questions like "Has the flag appeared yet?" This approach to paraphrasing keeps some of the "flavor" of the original.

Other paraphrasers try to capture the general meaning first. They give up the questions (on the grounds that they aren't real questions anyway), and for the sake of clarity they give up the other familiar patterns of the original: "I hope the flag still flies over this country." These paraphrasers do their best work in relating the meaning of the original to meanings in today's world. They might also find their version much shorter than the original.

Neither way of paraphrasing is wrong or right, of course. Each has its strength and weakness. There is probably no way to capture both the general meaning and the specific "flavor" of one text in another, so paraphrasers will always have to make a hard choice between these two kinds of inadequacy. But the way you chose to paraphrase the Anthem says something about your natural approach to understanding a text: Did you look for a general meaning, or did you look for one-at-a-time equivalents? However you approached it, you had a style, a preferred way of "learning" the Anthem. One goal of this chapter is to help you become more fully aware of that style.

AN EXAMPLE OF SUCCESSFUL LEARNING

A close look at your favorite ways of learning can make you a more effective learner. Also, you can help others become more effective learners by making your strategy clear to them. Chances are that other people in your class will find your method a useful variation on their favorite methods, provided that you can explain it thoroughly enough. Chances are, too, that you can add to your own repertoire of effective strategies by reading what others write about their learning styles.

The writing activity that follows asks you to examine in detail— for yourself and for others in your class—how you developed a clear understanding of some situation outside of school that you had originally approached in ignorance or error. Your learning style is the topic of this section, and your analysis of that learning style is what makes this section work. It cannot succeed for you without you actively participating in this activity. In fact, much of the quality of your experience in your writing course depends on the quality of your participation.

A writing course is the perfect place for you to review your learning strategies, identify their strengths and weaknesses, and begin to take control of their development. All books ask you to learn, but this book will also ask you to learn how you learn. All your life you will be learning, and, with your help, this book should contribute to that learning by making you more aware of how you can do it best.

ACTIVITY 1–2: LEARNING

This activity, like many others in this book, could form the basis of an essay. If you are assigned or choose to write such an essay you can follow the directions in Generating Material and Drafting below, then find out from your instructor what requirements of form your essay should meet. Further suggestions can be found at the end of the activity.

Generating Material

The first part of this task is to identify a learning experience that went well for you outside of school. Choose one that went beyond the simple acquisition of new information to overcome some deficiency or problem or bring about a significant and lasting change in your behavior. (If you write about some learning experience that didn't have this impact, you risk having little to contribute to your own sense of how you can learn best.)

To avoid rushing this step, you might want to list several possible examples of learning and then choose among them: in a sport, perhaps some particular move or skill that brought confidence or success; in a hobby, a new technique or other breakthrough; or in personal relations, facing some truth or some difficulty such as moving away from home and learning to take care of yourself. You might also want to get someone else's opinion about the possible examples—which would be the most likely to show something useful about learning that might otherwise be overlooked?

Once you have chosen the learning experience you will write about, the next step is to imagine fully what you were like before it. This is hard. You may have invested a lot of time and energy in becoming different from this "before" stage, and you may have buried it under lots of other thoughts and actions. Make notes to yourself about some of your actions and their consequences before the learning experience took place—the more specific the better.

Then identify in notes, again as concretely as you can, what prompted the change. What made you see the need to learn or become different? Was it some goal you were pursuing? Someone's perception of you? What motivation led you to want to change?

Next, as best you can, reconstruct the learning itself. Did you begin with alternatives, or did you have only a single path to follow? Were there identifiable steps? Was it a case of steady progress; instant success; or one step forward, one step back, two steps forward, and so? Were these setbacks or relapses? Do you remember a point at which you realized you were going to succeed?

Your last step in generating material for this paper is to look at the role the learning has since played in your life. Have you continued the activity? Do you still feel the temptations of the old ways? Can you identify other traces of the experience, other consequences, or other impacts?

If you are the kind of writer who likes to get opinions on what you are doing before drafting a version of your paper, now might be a good time to ask someone about what you are going to write— does it make sense generally? Does it raise questions that will need to be answered? Does it fall naturally into clearly separate sections?

Drafting

Write a draft of the paper as you would like others' papers to be written. As a reader, you want to know how other people went about their learning, and you would want enough detail so that you could learn to do what they did. You would also want that detail organized in manageable sections so that you don't get lost as you read it. Try to set up your draft to accomplish these same goals for your readers.

If you are assigned or if you choose to revise this draft into an essay, you will need to pay close attention to shaping it for the requirements of readers. They will not necessarily know why you are writing, for one thing, so they will need to be told early what your point is and why it matters. Then they will want to know what experience you have that supports your view. These are not arbitrary requirements. They come from the natural curiosity of readers like you, who might very well improve their learning by hearing about yours. You may have additional requirements to meet as well.

LEARNING FROM OTHERS

The activity (Activity 1–3) in the next section of this chapter will ask you to compare your learning experience with another person's. There are two reasons for thinking this comparison will be useful; one is specific, and is discussed in the next section. The one discussed here applies to this book as a whole.

One of the richest resources in your writing class is the other people in it, not just the teacher but the teacher plus all the other students. This is not the usual way to regard the other students in your class. Much of your education may have been competitive; if you are graded on a curve in some class, you know that helping someone else could hurt your own marks. Or perhaps you feel that others in the class cannot be of any use to you because they don't know any more about the subject than you do.

These objections have weight. Academic competition is a fact of life, and so is the lack of skill you might attribute to others. Nevertheless, advanced learners such as graduate students, law students, or science students assigned to laboratories routinely cooperate, setting up study groups, working groups, or project groups. What do they know that makes them do this?

They know of course that learning is finally an individual matter. No one does your learning for you, and no one else does it in exactly the same way that you do. Given even the best notes in the world, law students still must learn to *use* those notes to do well, and using them is something they figure out how to do on their own.

But good learners also know that in another way learning is a social matter, dependent on other people. A grad student assigned to a biochemistry lab, for example, is only as good as the other people who work on other parts of the experiment. In all fields of knowledge and most fields of work, people collaborate.

As in other fields, learning to write is ultimately an individual matter, despite the best help in the world, and yet it will proceed more efficiently if the learner has the maximum of assistance from as many readers and commentators as possible. It is therefore in all writers' interest to draw on the writers around them.

You need to work properly with the people around you, of course, to get the most out of them. They can substitute for a general audience, for an educated audience, for a friendly audience, or for a critical audience, depending on how you and your teacher approach them. If you write for them, and if you consider them as an important audience—as important as your teacher—you will get better practice. They might not be impressed by what impresses a teacher, or they might recognize a cliché that the teacher misses. They might be less sympathetic than a teacher or less willing to excuse you for making them struggle to find a meaning in some unclear wording. In many ways, they keep you honest, or they can. One way or another, however, you should consider them an opportunity to get an honest response to your writing that will hurt much less than someday having your boss tell you to redo a memo—or worse.

An indirect goal of this chapter, in fact, is to help make your class a good place to learn, a successful learning environment. But this can occur only when all members of the class realize two things: that they learn better together than apart and that they can gather and synthesize information more effectively than a single student or even a single student and teacher together. The success of the whole group depends on the benefit each person gains from the work of others. In this exercise, just hearing how others learn *anything* can give you new ways to learn the things you want to learn, making you more flexible as a learner. By understanding the categories into which learners can be grouped, you can learn to choose among the different ways of learning. The generalizations you draw about those categories can give you the resources to become a lifelong active learner. A successful learning environment allows all to experience the genuine utility of others' views.

European universities were cooperative in this way when they began a millennium ago. Groups of students hired the faculty, decided when they had learned what they wanted, evaluated one another's performance, and in general regulated their own learning environments. Although the power relations may have changed, the opportunity still remains for students to direct their own learning if they choose to make that learning truly effective.

YOUR LEARNING CONTRASTED WITH OTHERS'

In the preceding section, I have argued that you can learn from other students in many ways. In this section, you can try one specific way. You will compare your learning experience with someone else's.

One of the goals of the following activity is to help you consider the points of comparison you might use, rather than simply taking the first few that occur to you. (The detail you wrote in Activity 1–2 was meant to allow a wider range of possible contrasts.) This is the way comparison-and-contrast writing generally works when you do it after leaving school. The areas or points of comparison are often your responsibility, not assigned by the person who wants your report as to which of two proposals would be preferable. You have to argue not only that one plan is cheaper but that cost should be (or should not be) the overriding consideration. Perhaps you argue for the more expensive plan because you see its advantages in some other areas—future flexibility, public relations, ethics. You must create the areas of consideration, in addition to scoring the proposals in those areas, and you must weigh the areas in accord with the importance you think they have. These tasks are what Activity 1–3 asks for.

ACTIVITY 1–3: COMPARING LEARNING

Task

Using your draft from Activity 1–2 about a learning experience and your readings of other people's drafts, compare and contrast your own and any other person's learning. (A sample comparison is discussed after this activity.)

Background

If you were reading a comparison of this kind, you'd expect to find more than the usual familiar categories because of those you already know. You already know that some learners are faster than others, that subject matter makes a difference to learning, that the age of the learner is important. Such things are obvious, and wouldn't interest you much. As a writer, be wary of insulting your readers by telling them things that they already know.

Another preliminary consideration is that you and the person with whom you compare may have had different ideas about what learning is. You may need to develop a definition that covers both kinds in order to do the comparison, and you might find that this is not easy to do. If you wrote about teaching yourself to change a tire and your partner wrote about learning to value her best friend properly, your definition skills may get a workout. But without the definition, your comparison would bring together two things that were too unlike to tell readers much.

Drafting

Writing for readers like yourself, then, you will want to make clear what you think learning is (what the two examples of learning have in common), and you will want to isolate at least three differences. You will want to explain why you think these are the right points of contrast to bring out. You may also want to say something about why the comparison is important; in general, the idea is that a comparison of any pair may turn up essential elements of learning that other comparisons may miss, but what specifically have you found and why does it matter?

Notes

This way of using earlier writing as a basis for later writing is what writers mean by "revision." When you revise in this way, you literally *re-see* what you have done before, from a completely different point of view or for a completely different purpose. Many writers find this the most valuable part of writing, because they discover things in revising that they did not know they knew the first time around. You may find that some parts of your first draft about your own learning are no longer useful, given the comparison. This is an important experience. I suggest that you not throw away altogether the parts that do not fit. Most writers find that material they discard from one piece of writing has a way of turning up somewhere else. But temporarily putting that material aside seems to call for a self-discipline we all need more of.

TWO EXAMPLES OF LEARNING

For a sample of what Activity 1–3 can lead to, I will use a personal comparison, because I have found it very difficult to compare other people's learning unless I know at least one side of the comparison from the inside. The first time I wrote about learning along the lines of Activity 1–2, I wrote about learning to keep my emotions under control while scuba diving. The following six paragraphs are a brief version of that writing:

I was a beginner at diving but a good swimmer and in excellent physical condition. But I couldn't get as much time from a tank of air as other students. I would get so excited that I would breathe up all my air before my buddy was halfway through his. That made my buddies mad, and me, too. They called me "the airburner." I had expected scuba diving class to teach me the technology of diving, and it did. But now I found I had to learn some psychology along with the technology. I wasn't happy about that; in fact, I resented it. I was rude to everyone at this time; I felt isolated and frustrated. [I mentioned incidents.]

My instructors were no help at all; in fact, they made things worse. They bugged me about my problem, teased me about it, made jokes to each other about "that air-burner in the class." They pointed out that I would never be able to dive below about sixty feet safely, since I wouldn't have enough air to decompress adequately. On the beach one day, one of them said, "Why don't you forget the whole thing?"

At first I went through the usual stages of "Why me?" and of complaining that the diving program wasn't teaching me what I needed to know. Then it dawned on me that *they* didn't know either. None of them had faced the problem, in all likelihood. So it was up to me to solve my own difficulty.

After that, the worst was over. I knew what the problem was, and I could immediately think of some things to do about it, now that I had decided I was the one who had to. I was in good shape and able to swim long distances; I could swim fifty yards underwater easily, seventy-five or a hundred with a little effort. How did I do that? I hadn't been aware of it, but apparently I already knew some ways of controlling my breathing. I would calm myself down, relax, send my mind off to do something else, while my arms and legs gently propelled me as far as I wanted to go underwater.

The solution to my problem wasn't quite this simple, but essentially what I did was *find* the solution rather than invent a completely new one. I moved something I could already do into the situation where I wasn't getting the job done. After I became aware of what my way of relaxing was, I practiced using my relaxation and calming techniques with the scuba, first in a pool until I knew what it felt like, and then in the ocean.

By the end of my time in the diving program, I was an instructor myself. My specialty, of course, was people who got very excited about diving, who couldn't relax, who used up their air rapidly, or who were even inclined to panic. I had something to tell these people about emotional control because I had found it out for myself.

In writing out this experience in a draft, I became aware of one of my own favorite learning strategies, which is to bring to the problem something I already know how to do. I have used this same learning strategy in improving my writing: A teacher told me once that I talked better than I wrote, and so I began to use talking as a way to get papers going—discussing what I wanted to write with someone before writing it and also imagining as I wrote that I was talking to someone in particular.

That is *not* the only way to learn. It is *not* a way everyone learns. It happened to be the way I learned emotional control in scuba diving, and it showed me something about myself. When you know something just as concrete about how *you* like to learn, you can take similar advantage of this strategy in a writing class. It might mean, for instance, that you would draw on skills you already possess, as I did, but it might mean instead that you invent completely new skills for improving your writing.

In discussing this experience with others, I immediately found out that other people had their own favorite strategies. In fact, every paper I have read on this topic seems to have sharp contrasts

with the others. Looking for these contrasts seems to me the most
helpful way to read these papers, and it makes a group that shares
papers into a pioneering research group because all of us seem to
know more about our own learning than anyone else could and
because the comparisons quite often have never been made at the
level of detail we have in front of us. One example of a particularly sharp contrast to my learning style was that of a student
named Bob.

Bob wrote about learning to play chess. At the time he wrote
his paper, he had a high national ranking, although he was not
competing actively while in college. He wrote about learning to
play—not about learning the game but about becoming able to play
at the level he wanted.

> I learned fairly late for a chessplayer, in seventh or eighth
> grade. When I first learned, I got beaten hundreds of times. I
> remember once I lost to my friend Steve more than twenty
> times in a row one afternoon. I think ten times must have been
> exactly the same way, "Fool's Mate." It takes four moves.
>
> But I liked the game, and became determined to get better
> at it. Once when my father saw me playing a game with myself,
> he told me that one of our neighbors was a master player. He
> offered to ask the man if he would help me, and I said "okay."
> The man agreed, and we started right away. I think I was
> fourteen.
>
> We practiced openings, hour after hour. We practiced
> endgames, every combination and position. We reviewed great
> games from books, move by move. Every Saturday, I'd go over
> in the morning, about nine, and we'd practice and go over
> things and talk about moves and strategy. We'd have lunch, and
> play some games until three or four. Sometimes we would play
> on Wednesdays too. We would record each move of the actual
> games, and later I was supposed to check the moves against
> actual games that had started the same way, to see what we had
> done differently. I didn't always do that, in fact I didn't do it
> very much, because it was too slow.
>
> Over three years, bit by bit, I got better. Sometimes he
> would say I made a good move, or he would say, "Now you can
> finish this one by yourself, right?" In high school I began
> competing. When my teacher found out I was in a tournament,
> he taught me about eye contact, about how to look at the other

player's eyes to see what he was planning. Sometimes I could tell exactly. In my first tournament, I think it was C level, I didn't lose a game, and I drew and won enough to win the tournament.

I thought I was getting good enough to be on my own, but I continued the lessons for more than a year. Finally I was sure I was ready to go ahead by myself.

We both learned from the contrast between us. One point of comparison was our attitude toward people who knew more than we did. Some people—sometimes—prefer to learn from experts, the way that Bob learned chess, while others prefer to learn for themselves (at least sometimes). I think I would have learned to control my breathing from the scuba if I had been told, but I enjoyed the learning once I got started on it myself.

Some people are careful to examine all the precedents, all the alternatives, all the ways the thing can be learned, while others like to feel they are the first to try something. Some people like to be thorough and are content with gradual improvement, or are content only with slow growth, as Bob was, while others like swiftness and quick success. Some people like detailed solutions or strategies, while others like strategies that show outlines only, which then must be worked out. These contrasts told Bob and me both how to intensify or streamline our own methods and how to learn differently if we wanted.

Although many of us feel that our learning can be improved, we should also always remember that our successful learning happened in a certain way for a reason—because at that time and in those circumstances that was the way we should have learned. Satisfaction is the key; if we are satisfied with the learning, it was right for us. The point of comparing is not to change this satisfaction and most emphatically not to make us dissatisfied with the way we learn. Rather, the point is, first, to make us more aware of our own favorite ways of learning so that we can learn better in those ways. Next, it is to help us see possible alternatives so that we can become more flexible. Always, it seems that both sides of the contrast can lead to valuable insight.

Between any two papers, you can undoubtedly identify a long series of differences like those between Bob and me. If you have a third paper to examine, you can integrate it into your thinking by asking whether it is more like the first or the second and identifying the traits it shares with the others and those that are unique. This kind of comparison is the way psychologists of learning proceed, although they generally look for more abstract generalizations than a writing class would and are less interested in individual peculiarities than in patterns among learners. You have the advantage of being able to refer all your theories immediately to yourself because your paper has been one of the starting points.

KINDS OF LEARNING

The primary objective of this chapter so far has been to help you reflect on your favorite learning strategies. I hope that one or another of these strategies can help you learn to improve your writing. In this section, I'll try to show how some of these strategies might work for you.

If you are like Bob, you probably approach learning in a particular order—from small parts to the whole. For some people, this kind of approach to writing is the only strategy that works. (It is the kind of strategy that might appeal to you if you paraphrased the Anthem word by word.) You begin by practicing words and sentences, parts of speech, and types of sentences; you move later to a basic paragraph type, then expand to other paragraph types; and then you enlarge the paragraph structures into larger papers. Such an approach is common in textbooks, and your instructor can suggest a book for you to supplement your course if you ask, or you can find a self-paced textbook that works this way at your bookstore.

One trouble with such an approach to writing is that it is very time-consuming. A typical part-to-whole approach takes a year or more, and much of what you learn doesn't figure directly in the writing that you go on to do. So be warned that you will put out lots of extra effort if you follow this path—but *follow* it, if that is your preference. Make sure you keep writing large pieces while you work with the small parts of language—that mixture seems to lead to the best results because it helps to keep you from losing a sense of the whole of writing while you concentrate on the parts.

If you prefer a whole-to-part approach, you will have the opposite trouble. You will naturally spend time getting your purpose clear in your own mind as you write because that is the largest or "top" issue that a writer must face. And you'll spend time figuring out exactly why you care about a particular subject or what there is in it to care about; you'll also spend time figuring out how the large blocks of your paper should work. But in the execution of a plan for a paper, you may find that you aren't as much in control of the sentences and words as you would like to be. What should you do?

Such a difference in preferred learning styles is one of the best reasons for having writing taught in classes. In any class, there will be people who operate differently from you. You can learn from them. In my case, I learned from someone very much like Bob who helped me with the phrasings and grammar until I got enough under control to do my assignments successfully. I strongly recommend that you look for people to work with who are quite different from you. They will be better audiences for you to try your writing on because they don't see things exactly the way you do.

Another very common preference is for learning that is very active, even physical. Many people are quite comfortable learning a new physical skill because they know that they have talent in this area. They may like to get the look of a new gymnastic move first and the exact details later, or they might like to get the details first and the rhythm later. Can this preference be exploited?

There's not a lot you can do to make writing into a physical act, or course, but some carry-over is possible. You can "rehearse" your writing by discussing it with several different people in different circumstances; something about talking seems to help some people figure out what they want to say. Writers also speak of "dramatizing" their writing, of imagining it as the record of a conversation between two people, so that there is action in the words themselves.

A closer analogy is the idea of "exercises" that build your writing muscles. Keeping a journal of observations and reflections, writing minithemes out of the content of your other courses, freewriting, and other kinds of writing exercises can play the same role for writers that calisthenics or body-building workouts do for the physically fit. This kind of activity, in fact, is quite common among professional writers, each of whom seems to develop his or her own workout—so many words per day, or so many journal entries a week, for example. Like athletes, these writers like the idea of getting a little bit better every day, of straining against obstacles (such as trying to say what's *really* on your mind right now or writing just as fast as you can for a certain length of time). The advantage of this analogy is that it explains why after a layoff we often find we aren't writing as well as we used to, and it suggests why learning to write seems to be something we never quite get to the end of.

There is no way anyone but you can know what approach to writing is right for you. What distinguishes the better writers, more than talent or luck, is the willingness to take a personal approach to learning to write. Just as your own successful learning owed its success at least in part to your engagement with it, so your improvement in writing will benefit from the same kind of engagement. Adapting the classroom activities, or supplementing them, is the only reasonable path to take once you realize just how different all learners are.

WHAT IS LEARNING?

Most later chapters will provide an activity that invites you to assemble and summarize what you have done in the chapter. Here is my attempt to summarize this chapter and to say where I think it comes out.

By now, I've repeated the word "learning" so often that it might have begun to sound like an Anthem. A consequence of doing so is that we need to paraphrase the word. What is "learning," if this chapter's experiences are to be our guide?

It should be clear that learning is not filling an empty container. In every successful learning experience I have heard about, the learner was far from empty. In fact, many people report that a significant learning experience occurred at a time when they thought they were already "full." By "full" I mean that the learner already possesses skills, facts, a viewpoint, beliefs, plans, and so on; the learning that occurs seems often to come from rearranging or restructuring or re-seeing what is already there. But this doesn't mean that you must try to fill yourself up with skills or facts before you can learn. Instead, it seems to mean that learning is best seen as a kind of *inter*action between a self and material or experience. The successful learner seems always to meet the new with something relevant from the old.

Nor does successful learning imply an easy pouring of material into that container, empty or full. Sometimes successful learning is easy and sometimes it isn't, but even when it is easy, it seems always to require some resistance from the learner, some sense of an obstacle to overcome. Learning is wrestling, quite often, admitting doubts and uncertainties, finding inconsistencies, searching for connections or patterns, filling gaps and rearranging what's left.

Learning, we have said, is both *active* and *personal*. It is active in that the learner has to make the learning happen, and it is personal in that the learning is not necessarily the same for any two people. Learning is building, in a sense, or it is changing, by self-induced changes; that is what we seem to mean by *active*. And it is crafted for oneself; it is a matter of taking a stand on something or of deciding that one can do it, or of figuring out how one can connect to the thing to be learned.

In no sense, then, is learning a matter of submitting yourself to something, even if that is how it begins. Eventually you dominate it; the power is on the side of the learner. In mere memorization— the "Star-Spangled Banner" effect—there is no power on the learner's side which means that what is learned is either unexamined or useless or both.

Because learning is both active and personal, we can say that people *learn* to write, but no one is *taught* to write. The responsibility for learning to write rests entirely with the learner because of the very nature of the writing process, as we shall see in Chapters Two and Three. The more responsibility you take, the faster you will learn to write. This book, your course, other students—all can help, all can make useful ideas and practice available, but none can finally do it for you but yourself.

A final point about how people learn language skills. Twice in this chapter I have drawn on an analogy between writing skills and athletic skills, but all analogies break down somewhere, and this one does too. We say of people playing a sport that they are "unconscious," that they are relaxed and confident and not hindered by extra awareness of what they are doing. But people who are improving their ability to write (or speak or read or use language in some other way) generally say the opposite. They say they become *more* aware of what they are doing. As you paraphrased, you may well have noticed yourself working with the words of the Anthem or becoming ever more conscious of what it says and does. If your experience parallels many other people's, you will continue to build this awareness as you learn more about writing. Your learning will be smoother for it and your writing better as well.

CONCLUDING ACTIVITY: THE LAST WORD

In this chapter, you, the reader, have the last word. Now that you have heard about how other people learn, what changes might you want to make in your own learning style?

If you think some change might be useful, would it be desirable to intensify something you already do? Would some more radical change be in order? Could you make some adjustment in your learning style in school based on your learning style outside of school?

Write yourself a short proposal, suggesting the improvement you wish to make and estimating its chances of becoming a permanent part of your repertoire.

If you do not think change is a good idea at this time or if you are satisfied with your repertoire of learning techniques, you might think about a different and equally interesting question—how did you learn how to learn? Record for yourself as best you can (perhaps as a model for other people) how you became aware of the successful strategies you employ in learning.

CHAPTER 2

How People Read

THE POINT OF THIS CHAPTER

You can improve your reading by following some of the ideas of this chapter, and that might be a benefit in itself. But reading is important in a book about writing because much of what we write will be read. What readers actually do sets limits and also creates opportunities for writers.

What do people do when they read? Your experience in this chapter will enable you to develop some answers to this question so that, in the next chapter, we can investigate how writers can help readers do their reading better.

WHAT IS A GOOD READER?

Have you ever known an excellent reader? Perhaps you have heard about or even met somewhere a reader who seems to operate at superhuman speed. He or she tears off huge chunks of material at a time, reads whole books in a single day, has time not only for reading assignments but also for the recommended reading or extra credit work—even reads for pleasure—while the rest of us struggle to get through the reading we must do.

If you know about reading rates, you may think that such a person reads several times faster than the average, perhaps 2,000 words a minute instead of the 300 or 400 that most of us can manage. You may have seen the hand movements that go along with such rapid reading: gentle back-and-forth sweeps across pages that would get grubby and sweatstained if you or I held them. You may have seen the advertisements that suggest fast readers have time for social lives in addition to their studies—without guilt.

You probably "know" a bit more about such readers. Speed sets them apart, but other abilities seem to also. These readers are supposed to transfer information from the page into their heads better than you or I can do it. Where we have a "noisy channel" on our incoming line, theirs seems to be unimpeded. They aren't distracted by stray thoughts, by any difficulties in concentrating, or by conflict with other things they know or have read. The material just seems to "flow in" as if it were being recorded on a disk. When such people read, we suppose they aren't really working, because nothing seems hard, nothing makes them go back to reread, and nothing comes up to bother them about what they have read.

Perhaps you see such people assimilating the chunks and retaining material so well that they can reproduce it any time later almost word for word. We all have heard of cases of "photographic memory," in which a person can simply glance at pages of text and then, years later in some cases, close his or her eyes and "read off" from a mental page what was there, word perfect. For such readers, we suppose, recalling information must be like remembering the "Star-Spangled Banner," just a matter of getting the right starting word and rhythm to guarantee the flow of the whole text.

Finally, many of us have the idea that what separates us from such superreaders is effort. "If only I were willing to work a little harder at reading," we may think, "I too could read like that." Others of us may have the idea that we are underprivileged compared to such readers, born without the genetic makeup to become superreaders and consequently doomed to plod along all our lives.

This stereotype of the "good reader" is so widespread and so complete that it does a great deal of damage. There is actually much more to reading than this picture of superreaders pouring data into their heads. People who mumble to themselves as they read may be getting more out of a paragraph than rapid readers get from a chapter. Readers who go back over parts of what they have just read may get as much or more out of the second reading as a quick reader would out of the first and may develop a new way of thinking about what the page says. Staring off into space from time to time may be better for comprehension than simply plowing ahead and neglecting to connect with previous knowledge. Slow reading may be much more effective for many purposes than zipping through an article. There are many ways of being a good reader.

ACTIVITY 2–1: FILLING THE GAPS

To prepare for this activity, you will need to choose some expository writing, perhaps a chapter or section of a book or an article written at a level you think any college freshman should be able to read. It should be neither too familiar nor too easy. (A newspaper article is probably too easy). A book assigned in one of your classes or one of your textbooks might provide suitable material; you could also look in magazines that publish articles several pages long, either general ones such as *Scientific American, The Atlantic,* or *Harper's,* or more specialized ones, such as *Psychology Today, Money,* or *Consumer Reports.* Your selection might be from the beginning of the chapter or article; if it isn't, it should still seem fairly independent. You will need a passage of about 200 words—a bit less than a page.

Prepare a worksheet for other students in this way: Rewrite (preferably retype) the first sentence of your selection as it stands. Retype the first four words of the next sentence, and then, in place of the fifth word, type a blank of ten spaces, giving it the number 1. Type the sixth word, the seventh, eighth, and ninth, and then type in place of the tenth word another ten-space black, number 2. Continue in this way, replacing every fifth word with a blank, until you have thirty blanks. Be sure to make a copy of the original version so that you have an answer sheet. You will need from one to five or more photocopies of your exercise, depending on the size of the small group in which you are assigned to work.

The worksheet will look like this:

Suppose that a manufacturer of light bulbs produces roughly a half million bulbs per day. Concerned about customer reaction (1) _____ its product, the firm (2) _____ to determine the fraction (3) _____ bulbs produced on a (4) __

_____ day that are defective. (5) _____ can solve
the problem (6) _____ two ways. All of (7) _____
half million bulbs could (8) _____ inserted into sockets
and (9) _____ , but the cost of (10) _____ solution
would be substantial . . . (and so on, to thirty blanks).

From William Mendenhall and Lyman Ott, *Understanding Statistics*,
3d ed. (North Scituate, MA: Duxbury Press, 1980), 1.

Either in pairs or small groups, exchange worksheets. Fill each
blank on the worksheet you receive with a single word. This part of
the exercise will take between twenty and thirty minutes.

This kind of exercise works with what is called a CLOZE
passage. The name comes from Gestalt psychology, which looks at
how people complete or "close" their perceptions and experience.
CLOZE passages can be used to estimate the difficulty of a text if
you know how good a particular reader is. Also, if you want to know
whether a given group of people can manage the text as a whole,
you give them a CLOZE passage from it and see whether they can
replace half the blanks. This is the way teachers decide whether a
particular book is suitable for a class.

Filling half the blanks is a *perfect* score. This scoring is
sometimes hard for people to accept until they reflect on exactly
what completing a CLOZE passage involves. Some words really
cannot be anything else—as blank 1 above can hardly be anything
but the word "to." Some blanks will be almost impossible to fill—
as would happen in the above example if the name of the company
occurred only once and a blank replaced it. But many blanks are of
moderate difficulty, and these are the point of this CLOZE exercise.

THE ACTIVE READER

In analyzing the experience of a CLOZE exercise, we can't
avoid several conclusions. For one thing, well-written prose apparently contains so much repetition and overlap that we can read it
almost as well with 20 percent of it missing as we can with it all
there.

This first point seems significant in itself to many people who
thought before doing this exercise that in their own writing they

should try to reduce the repetition and overlap to zero. Perhaps in some poetry the redundancy approaches zero, and the next word is always pretty much unpredictable. Even then, however, we seem to need to be told things more than once in order to have our understanding of a piece of writing reinforced by more than one means.

In the example given above, the structure of the sentence tells us before we get to blank 1 that the word is "to." If we had been reading the original passage with no blanks, we would already know that the word "to" has to be where it is even before we get to it. Then, when we actually see the word, we are told *again* that it is "to," so we get confirmation that we really are reading correctly. This interplay of our expectations with the text goes on continually as we read, sometimes unbeknownst to us and occasionally in ways we notice, such as when we are trying extra hard to figure out something complicated. Because this confirmation of expectations is such a direct way of telling readers that they are reading properly, writers of expository prose are generally content that readers should already know many words before actually arriving at them.

Important as this point about writing is, a CLOZE experience reveals a still more important point about reading. Readers seem to have a built-in sensemaking faculty, an ability to fill in gaps. When activated by a blank, this ability can supply a missing item at least half the time for a text at one's reading level. More important, even when not activated by a blank, this ability can make of reading a far richer and more meaningful activity than simply pouring information into one's head. This ability, in fact, is the key to understanding what reading really is.

Readers make sense of what they read; in other words, readers make meaning. They read *actively*. They bring together the clues they get from the text, their previous experience with the topic and with the language in which it is written, their purpose in reading, and other elements. Readers assemble, estimate, predict, judge, extend, apply, guess, and paraphrase, to name only a few of the hundreds of things that readers can do. One characteristic of very skilled readers is the ability to notice what a writer is *not* saying, which amounts to creating a blank for oneself as one reads and then filling it.

The beliefs and opinions of active readers are naturally going to figure in their reading. What they take the words to be saying will shape the kinds of blanks they mentally create and fill, and they use past experience to fill the blanks they create. No writing can prevent this; readers who want to make sense in a certain way will do so. Readers therefore determine how much effect a piece of writing will have on them. Writers can supply materials and guidelines that indicate their preferred interpretation, but they cannot control completely what their readers will do.

This view of reading clearly has implications for writing. A good writer will not try to precook everything for a reader but instead will allow the reader to participate in the making of meaning. Chapter Three will present some way of doing this. To mention just one here, we might remember the old advice that good writers should "show, not tell." That advice is often good because showing lets a reader draw conclusions, while telling challenges a reader to disagree with a writer's conclusions.

In the meantime, however, we should return to look at the myths about reading with which we began. What looked like skilled reading—speed, ease, exact recall—now looks like taking the easy way out, avoiding the real task of reading. No matter how fast you do it, if you read a piece of writing simply to try to absorb it, you are reducing the activities you could be engaging in and you are reducing the value the writing can have for you. You will eventually have to face the "Star-Spangled Banner" effect, the effect of finding out that a text you "know" in some superficial sense has in fact been virtually a blank for you.

All books are really workbooks. All provide opportunities for readers to fill in gaps, supply connections, notice what's missing, and so on. People who read very rapidly are simply passing up these opportunities, choosing to get an overall sense of the work without actually doing anything very active. For some purposes, that kind of skimming is useful. For other purposes, it just wastes time.

This idea of reading is unusual and counterintuitive, of course. We generally think of a book as a container, filled with knowledge as a milk carton is filled with milk, waiting to be poured into us. But it helps readers (and writers) more to think of a book in a different image, as a set of pieces and rules for playing a game. The game must be used in order to come to life; we don't know the game until we have played it. A book is an experience waiting to happen.

READING AND LEARNING

Reading seen in this way is very much like the account of learning presented in Chapter One. Reading and learning are better, more useful, longer lasting, when we do them actively, when we change meanings into our own words, when we check our expectations about what is coming next with what actually comes next, when we keep in mind our purposes and the strengths we have displayed in previous learnings or readings.

And writing, of course, is teaching. If you don't like teaching that tells you every detail of what to think, you won't like writing that tells you what to think either. Writing that leaves room for a reader to do something may be more attractive to more readers.

ACTIVITY 2–2: FIFTY SPECIFICS

The point of this activity is to do some writing that leaves *lots* of room for readers to participate. You can develop it into an essay if you wish by using the feedback explained at the end of the activity as a guide for revision.

The task is to try out a particular writing process to see whether you like it. In this writing process, your material determines the structure and direction of your writing while you try simply to provide enough detail for your readers to have a certain kind of experience if they choose. Since this process is meant to be a bit different from the way we ordinarily do things, you will see more of a contrast with your usual writing if you follow the directions closely.

Procedure

The first step is to choose an area of experience with which you are very familiar. It might be some part of a job, a hobby, or your daily routine. It does not have to be an area you are excited about, provided only that you know it very well. You can write about a bus ride you take daily if you have observed it very closely. You can write about a recent car repair you performed if you have a specific one in mind. You can write about a particular game you played recently (one you watched may not do as well unless you are a very keen observer). You can write about a car trip with a small child or some other experience with a member of your family.

The second step is to generate fifty specific points about this area of experience. No sentences are required at this point, since they will come later. The only trick is to be specific enough: after you have written out five or eight points, stop and choose one of them about which you can think of ten, twenty, or a whole set of fifty *more* specifics (an example is given below).

You cannot be too specific in this exercise. You may feel at first that being more specific makes generating points more difficult, but most people who try the activity find that just the reverse is true. The area you are writing about is familiar, and your memory most likely stores an extraordinary wealth of detail about it, although you might not be used to thinking of it in concrete terms. This activity is a little like figuring out how to describe the way you drive a car, or walk, or serve a tennis ball (and these would do for subjects). We often do these things automatically unless we try to teach someone else how to do them, and then we must focus on these details. Retrieving the details can bring the activity to life, both for us and for our readers.

Suppose you decide to write about the butterfly stroke in swimming. You then take seriously the instruction to choose a very familiar side of it, some specific occasion or event in which it figures. You decide to talk about teaching it to someone in a class recently. You generate some of these points:

teaching Sam the stroke
body position
kick
arm movement
rhythm
breathing

Then you choose one of these points under which to generate your fifty specifics:

teaching Sam
Sam begins the kick holding to side of pool
Sam bends knees too much, 90 degrees or more
much splash, no power
ankles flex properly
toes close together
heels apart
knees about 8–10 inches apart
got Sam out onto the pool deck to kick

held feet for a kick so he could feel it
(and so on)

It may be that your fifty specifics will cover only the kick practice! Surprisingly, however, readers are almost never bored by such a small topic (although they might question your purpose). If you are able to focus on your material at this level of detail, you will almost surely go more deeply into it than most other people have gone, and at that level you can tell readers something that they do not know. People are curious, of course; they can also tell from the level of detail that you care about the subject at least enough to have observed it closely, and that is a reason for them to care about it too. In fact, small topics do not bore readers so often as generality and abstractness do.

As you generate the list, keep asking, "Can I be more specific about that last item? Can I give five more specifics for *it*?"

The person who taught me this exercise taught himself to start writing this way about his hobby of sailing. He has since published more than thirty articles about sailing, not because he is a great sailor but because he is an excellent observer of sailing, able to give his sailor-readers new ways of looking at their common experience. (He revises a lot, as you might expect.)

Once you have a satisfactory list, look for the natural groups of items. The details of the kick example mentioned earlier might be arranged chronologically—what I did first, second, and third, or what I noticed first, second, and third. But they might also be arranged in order of importance—Sam's knee bend was too great, and that would prevent him from progressing unless I fixed it, but body position was a possible cause of the knee bend, so I worked on that the most; the other details stay together in a group of things he was doing right or in another group of things he was doing that didn't matter. There are no rules for making these groupings except to follow your instincts and knowledge.

The last step in the activity is this: Once you have made your groups of points, turn them into groups of sentences. If you feel you need paragraph breaks, use them.

Reading

Once you have written your fifty-specifics draft, exchange it with someone in your class. As you *read* someone else's specifics paper, notice what you do. At what point in the draft does the organization into groups become clear? How are you reacting to this level of detail? What is your impression of the writer? Do you trust the writer more than you usually would? Do you have to fill any gaps? Notes on these matters can help the writer revise later.

The writing that you do in this activity will be limited in that it won't give your readers much guidance. You might want to revise with this in mind if you are going to write an essay based on it. Unless you make a special effort to say something about why your topic is significant or why it demonstrates some idea or value you consider important, you can only hope that your readers will be interested. In some cases, writing to inform is enough of a purpose to elicit a favorable response from readers; we do seem to have a certain hunger for information that is factual and quite concrete. But there are real limitations to this kind of writing, which we will examine in the section on reading and purpose.

The fifty-specifics papers show that writing can work when it allows readers to participate in the making of meaning. Even with very minimal organization, such a paper can interest and inform a reader. We can combine this point with the point made by CLOZE passages in this way: Good writing takes advantage of the ways readers naturally make sense of what they read.

Although reading looks like an individual activity, then, it is in fact social through and through. You can usefully think of reading as a conversation or, more properly, a conversation on a stage. When you read, you take your place in a drama: You place yourself in a scene in which you also place your version of the writer. Both characters have pasts, and they have purposes. You decide what you will do and say as you see what the writer does and says. The writer provides half the dialogue and the stage directions, while the reader provides the other half of the dialogue and figures out how things are actually going to look on the stage. The play requires the active participation of both writer *and* reader. Writers provide the framework in which readers make things they didn't know before become real.

This reading environment need not remain in your head. In writing class, the "reading conversations" that usually go on in our heads can be spoken aloud, and we can add new voices to our dramas by noticing what others say about something they have read. We will return to this point in the concluding activity (Activity 2–4) for this chapter.

READING AND PURPOSE

Do you ever read to have your mind changed? Few of us do. Most of us are willing to have our knowledge extended, but not many of us pick up a book hoping that it will show us we've been wrong about something. When we detect an overt persuasive purpose, even if we are sympathetic, we tend to resist. As readers, we don't like to be pushed around. We will explore the implications of this characteristic for writers in Chapters Three and Five. Before examining those implications, however, we need to explore how readers identify and respond to writers' purposes.

ACTIVITY 2–3: AN ANTHOLOGY

One of the most sensible ways to use a large group of people, such as a class in writing, is as a research team. This activity asks you to use your class as a resource to gather information on the purposes exhibited in a wide variety of writing.

Each person in your research group (a small group or the whole class) should bring in two pieces of writing that are not fictional. This kind of writing is generally labeled "expository," which means "making plain" or "exposing." But within the general purpose of making something clear are many other purposes, and the aim of this activity is to explore them.

The writings should each be a page or more long, 250 words or more, and their purposes should be as different from each other as possible. You will need enough copies for each member of your working group.

Some sources of writing that would be helpful include business reports, memos, notices to specific audiences, technical reports, editorials, and sales literature. The more unusual your source, the more help it is likely to be. You might also use this activity to start investigating your probable or possible major or career: What kinds of writing will you have to produce and comprehend? Ask someone more advanced in your field for some samples of writing from it.

When the group has assembled and each person has contributed copies of two pieces of writing, the writings should be distributed to every member of the group. This collection or anthology will contain writings with a wide range of purposes. The first task is to agree on the purpose of each piece in as much detail as possible: Is it to tell a purchaser how to install a new smoke alarm? Is it to notify residents of a change in building policy? Is it to inform (really to inform, without *any* persuasive tinge)?

To perform an effective analysis, everyone must know how each piece of writing signals its purpose. Does it announce its purpose in so many words: The purpose of this letter is to inform you that . . . ? Or is the purpose less clear, perhaps given away by a few words that indicate someone is trying to sell something? Do not pass over any piece until you know what the purpose is and *how* it is signaled in the writing.

The next task is to sort these purposes into categories, name them, and then try to decide whether other categories have been left out. Either individually or in groups, you can make this task easier by comparing: Start on one piece of writing you are familiar with and compare it with a second to see how their purposes are alike and how they are different. (The anthologies will be useful in later chapters, so please save them.)

The purposes of writing are all but infinite in number because each purpose is the writer's precise aim for a particular audience about a limited subject. So here is a collection just of some *verbs* that a writer might use in stating an expository purpose: inform, relate, connect, identify causes, report, summarize, present evidence (for or against), argue for, raise doubts about, express oneself, present a (new) view of, oppose, support, evaluate, recommend, suggest, examine, analyze, clarify, present solutions, identify problems, expose, interpret, remind, place in perspective, notice, make a remark, reply, repeat, propose, sell, request, try to persuade, teach, object, smear, describe, narrate, offer thoughts on, show why, work out consequences, review, give the feeling of, show off, attract attention, confuse, obscure, conceal, mislead, inspire, cheer up, depress, entertain, submit to evaluation, impress, concede, imply, attack, defend, hasten, slow down.

But such a long list is not really as chaotic as it seems at first. Some of these purposes are much like other ones. The category into which your purpose falls offers a real and useful shortcut to help you identify more clearly what you are trying to accomplish as a writer. The clearer you are about your purpose, the more easily you will find the means to support and develop it.

WHAT READING IS REALLY LIKE

The CLOZE experience, the fifty-specifics writing and reading, and the examination of the anthology for purposes should provide you with a sharpened sense of what reading is really like. Reading is seldom a neutral, fill-up-your-empty-head kind of activity. More often, readers have a purpose in mind that helps them make sense of things; some readers can participate actively in their reading by looking for purposes, making extensions, finding gaps, trying to experience what is being talked about, comparing what is actually written with their expectations—helping to create meaning.

Reading thus has close connections with learning. In Chapter One, we examined our experiences to show how personal and active learning is. Here in Chapter Two, we have seen that reading is also personal and active.

In the next chapter, we will look further at the consequences for writing of these two sets of ideas: A writer is a teacher, but a teacher of unusually active pupils.

CONCLUDING ACTIVITY: YOU AS A READER

The point of this exercise is to enable you to analyze yourself as a reader.

In Activity 1–3, you wrote about a successful learning experience of your own and someone else's in order to define learning and compare strategies. Now trade that writing with someone else in your class and read the paper you receive.

Read it as actively as you can. As you read, keep track of everything that comes into your mind. You can do this by writing a sentence in response to every sentence that is in the paper, by questioning every step the writer seems to take, by paraphrasing, by raising every conceivable objection ("we already know this" and "no one could argue with that" are also objections), by thinking

aloud into a recorder as you read and then transcribing what you
have said in reaction, or by using other methods you develop
yourself. It is important to *have* a method.

Before returning the paper and your comments to the other
person, draft a paragraph about yourself as a reader to introduce
your comments. Base the paragraph on what you have just done in
the comments. Are you an easygoing, agreeable sort of reader? Are
you the kind of reader who likes all connections spelled out so you
miss nothing? Are you a hypercritical, go-for-the-jugular sort of
slasher? Are you the kind who likes to wrestle with each part? Do
you look for an overall message, or do you react word by word?
How would you characterize yourself based on your response to
this paper?

A FINAL NOTE: READING ACTIVELY

How do people read? We don't all read as actively as we can,
of course. But reading is still an activity, still a performance, even
if all we do is wonder what will come next. The more actively we
read—by asking questions, filling gaps, objecting, wondering why
the writer chose some word over another—the more we benefit. We
benefit by remembering—we remember what we do. We benefit by
coming to own the material ourselves—because we have made it.
We benefit by applying it—because we know what it can do.

LEARNING TO WRITE FOR READERS

In the next three chapters, you will be looking at how writers meet the needs of active readers, how they develop useful writing processes, and how they learn to write or to improve their writing.

In working with these chapters, you will have the chance to hear about how many other people actually learn to write, learn to generate material and shape it to meet the expectations of audiences. In Chapter Four, to begin with, you will hear about a variety of ways to find something interesting to write about and also about ways to develop your interests into material that people will want to read. As you read the rest of Part Two, you will become aware of ways in which you can take a piece of writing from its very beginnings, before you even know what you want to write, and take it through a draft, or even two, in which you find out what you want to say. As you read and work with the activities of Part Two, write a draft of an essay that you might like to revise later.

CHAPTER 3

How People Write— for Readers

THE POINT OF THIS CHAPTER

In this chapter, we begin finding out how writers can meet the needs of readers. How do we as writers convey what we want to convey while still allowing readers to make their own meaning?

In Chapter Two, we have just seen ways in which readers can be quite active. They make sense of things, they make meaning, they take over the text in a sense, and they use what they read for their own purposes. They fill in the gaps they find, even when the writer didn't intend to leave any gaps.

In these ways, readers pose problems for writers. How do writers "play percentages," choose the words that have the greatest chance of getting readers to make meanings like those the writer intends? In this chapter, we try to see how writers can write better for active readers.

WRITING AS CONVERSATION

As we have seen, because of the active nature of readers, it is important to think of writing as more like a conversation than a monologue. Readers seem almost free to do as they please, as free in some ways as they would be in a conversation: free to disagree, take a different view of things, form their own opinions, listen to only part of what the other person says, and leave if they lose interest.

ACTIVITY 3–1: READING AND CONVERSATION

Preparation

One of the basic rules of conversation is that people take turns. This activity asks you to follow that rule as you read to see how writing creates an *implied reader*, a ghostly ideal reader who always does what the writer wants, who always asks the right question that the writer goes on to answer. You will have the chance to read a writing sample one small piece at a time, asking a question after each piece to anticipate what the writer is going to say next in the conversation. You will also give someone else the same experience.

Procedure

Choose a piece of expository prose from a magazine or book, as you did in Activity 2–3. It could come from the same source but probably shouldn't come from exactly the same place because others in your group might realize that they have seen the text before, which will interfere with their anticipation.

Prepare worksheets for the activity by putting each sentence from the article on its own sheet of paper. Start with the title on a single sheet (or supply a section title); then write the first sentence on another sheet, the second sentence on another, and so on through 10–12 sentences, which will probably be not more than two paragraphs. Number the sheets for the convenience of your fellow students. These worksheets will be the "script" for the "conversation."

Before you receive your worksheets from someone else, think in a general way about what you expect from expository writing, based on Activity 2–3 or any of your previous reading. For example, you expect the writing to have a definite purpose: to report something, to explain how something works or interpret something mysterious, to evaluate or recommend something, to show the significance of something, and so on. You expect to find out fairly early the plan of the whole piece of writing. You have a right to have unclear or unusual terms defined briefly before they are used, or at least as soon as they are used. You expect certain kinds of development, especially those using examples. These are some of the expectations most of us have; you might have more or different ones. If you keep these expectations in mind or have them written down in front of you as you do this activity, you will ask sharper questions.

When you receive the worksheets, ask a question after you read each page, and write the question underneath the title or sentence you have just read. Next, read the following page and go back a page to write the question the author actually answers (the implied reader's question). Then go on to write your next question under the second sentence you have read. Continue until you have finished the worksheets. See my example below. When you come to the end, each sentence should have a pair of questions, one that you asked originally and one that the author actually went on to answer in the next sentence.

Reflection

Examine the contrast between the two questions in each pair closely. How close was your response to that of the implied reader? How do you account for the similarities and differences? Do you see possibilities for improving your reading? Do you see ways in which the writer could have better clarified his or her intentions?

Example

Here is an article that I have analyzed according to this "conversational" method. The whole article actually begins like this:

Telescience. The term is used by NASA to refer to scientific research conducted with computers and instruments connected by networks over great distances. It includes the remote design of experiments on space platforms, the operation of those experiments, and the collaboration of scientists around the world in interpreting and publishing results. The next best thing to being there, telescience is expected to be a common mode of research in all scientific fields by the mid-1990s.

For the safety and integrity of their research, experimenters want to be certain that they are linked to their own instruments when they request connections and that no one else can connect to those instruments. They want to be certain that no one can alter the data transmitted from their instruments, or the authorized commands sent to the instruments. They want to be certain that proprietary communications with their co-workers cannot be disclosed. The first guarantee, called authentication . . . .

From Peter J. Denning, "Security of Data in Networks," *American Scientist* 75, 1 (Jan.–Feb. 1987):12–14.

But I didn't see that opening all at once. Instead, I had a friend prepare a worksheet showing first the title, then the rest of the first two paragraphs sentence by sentence. After I read each sentence, I wrote a question or questions based on what I thought the writer would discuss next, then the question I found the writer had actually gone on to answer (the implied reader's question).

Here is an excerpt from my worksheet:

1. *Title*: "Security of Data in Networks"

   My question: From what I have read about computer raiders, how can data possibly be protected at all?

   The implied reader's question: What is the general domain in which the question of security needs examination?

   Comment: As you can see, I wasn't quite expecting what I got. The writer seemed to be taking a less direct path.

2. *First sentence*: "Telescience."

   My question: What *is* telescience? How could there be science at a distance? And what does telescience have to do with security anyway?

The implied reader's question: What is telescience?

Comment: Here at least I did get what I expected.

3. *Second sentence*: "The term is used by NASA to refer to scientific research conducted with computers and instruments connected by networks over great distances."

   My question: Why is security of more concern in that setting than in ordinary computer communication?

   The implied reader's question: What would be some examples of telescience?

4. *Third sentence*: "It includes the remote design of experiments on space platforms, the operation of those experiments, and the collaboration of scientists around the world in interpreting and publishing results."

   My question: Okay, so why is security an issue there?

   The implied reader's question: What is the significance of this research (and be a little bit amusing in your answer)?

5. *Fourth sentence*: "The next best thing to being there, telescience is expected to be a common mode of research in all scientific fields by the mid-1990s." (End of paragraph.)

   My question: Now tell me why security is an issue there?

   The implied reader's question: Why is security important there and what exactly does it require?

6. *Fifth sentence, new paragraph*: "For the safety and integrity of their research, experimenters want to be certain that they are linked to their own instruments when they request connections and that no one else can connect to those instruments."

As you can see, the author wasn't quite as ready to explain the issue as I had expected him to be, probably because he knew better than I did the complexity of the situation in which security is important and because he wanted to delay taking up the issue until he had given a sketch of the background I needed to understand the gravity of his issue. The implied reader was more patient, but otherwise we were much alike. Because I felt like one of the intended readers for this article, I was ready to continue reading it, but I had to be patient with this writer, whose pace was more deliberate than I had expected.

The conversational view of writing implies that writers need to observe many of the same guidelines that people observe in conversation. When you are talking to someone, you engage the other person's interest, you say clearly things that are relevant (or signal a change of topic), you say as much as is required, you try to make sure that the other person can follow your words, you say only what you believe or know to be true, and so on. These rules of conversation apply to writing as well. If you are too aggressive, you will drive readers away. If you are too defensive ("Of course it's only my opinion . . . "), people will wonder why they should pay attention. If you go on too long, people will lose interest.

But there are differences between writing and conversation that are just as obvious as the similarities. Writers don't usually have the advantage of seeing the expressions on their readers' faces that would tell how the conversation is going; that is why many writers get people to read their drafts in order to improve them. And, readers don't have the advantage of being able to deflect a conversation in midstream; they *must* either take it or leave it. This means that writers must take special care to construct their half of the conversation in ways that are fair, attractive, interesting, obviously useful, and easy to follow.

It is harder to make your writing easy to follow than your speech. When you are talking, you can tell immediately when someone doesn't understand you, and you can explain again, or change your words, or spell things out in greater detail. When you write, you must decide ahead of time just how much detail you need, how clearly you must connect one point to the next, how explicit you must be about such things as purpose, material, structure, grounds, and support.

No wonder, then, that it takes some time to learn to write—especially when each group of readers has different standards—and no wonder that professional writers say that they go on learning to write all their lives. These differences between conversation and writing mean that you must try to predict what other people will do, but people are predictable only to a limited extent. People change. Different groups of people behave differently. All these familiar and obvious facts affect the task of learning to write better and make it more difficult.

The rules of conversation that also apply to writing—be relevant, be efficient, be clear, and so on—are merely *general* advice about how to write for active readers. We can learn more specific strategies by looking at *ideas* and *structure*.

IDEAS AND OPINIONS

When you filled in the blanks in a CLOZE activity, you relied on past experience with what writers usually mean. When you took apart a piece of writing as a conversation, you saw how it takes two people to make a text. In both activities, you were experiencing the social dimension of reading and writing. Ideas, also, have a social dimension.

Seeing ideas in this way might be a little uncomfortable. We are accustomed to thinking of ideas as private property because they occur in our minds where other people cannot see them. Only we know what our own ideas are. And the strong sensation of "getting an idea" makes us feel that there must be something there that we get.

But this view of ideas also makes them seem rather mysterious and uncontrollable. We have all felt the thrill of getting an idea, but we have also felt the despair of being without an idea, of thinking and thinking and coming up empty, of having nothing to say. Being without an idea in a situation where we need one wouldn't be so bad if we had ways of arriving at ideas. Unfortunately, there aren't reliable paths for getting all-new ideas. Poets used to speak of a "muse," a spirit who would come and speak in their ear to tell them what to write, and this concept of a muse was useful, fictional though it was, because it helped relieve the terrible pressure to come up with something new. We also tend to think that younger people can't have ideas because they haven't had any experience and haven't learned enough "facts" to give them the necessary foundations for their out-of-the-blue thoughts.

A more helpful view of ideas is that they are shared. We can say that two people produce one idea, especially when they reach some conclusion that neither could have reached alone. If we see ideas as the results of conversation and interaction between people rather than as the property of a single individual, we can begin to ease the burden of writers. Writers don't have the burden of creating a whole and complete idea absolutely from the beginning. Instead, they supply at most half of the ingredients for an idea, which the reader completes and fills out.

Take the case of a business report, for example. The conclusion, which is said to embody the writer's idea, can be useful in itself even if the supervisor doesn't read the rest of the report. But the writer's real contribution is the development of that conclusion out of existing practices and research. The body of the report shows *how* the ideas (which may have been floating around the office for weeks as hypotheses, suggestions, or out-and-out fantasies) fit with things that lots of people in the company know through evidence and reasoning. The supervisor can read that section if needed. The writer of the report might have included genuinely new ideas in the report, but even these didn't occur in a vacuum; instead, they occured in the surroundings of other people's ideas and generally available evidence.

Some people are bothered by the view that they are writing "just their own opinions." The word "opinion" is usually derogatory, meaning a personal view, unsupported, without evidence, subjective, perhaps intuitive and not very logical, more closely related to feelings than to thought. It is a label, a way of putting down a view or a claim—or of protecting it from others who presumably don't care to try to change something so private as an opinion.

But "opinion" is another name for a "view," a "perspective," a "conclusion"—or "an idea." All these words describe the result of a person's examination (with more or less care and attention to detail) of some event or thing or state of affairs. We tend to use the word "opinion" to characterize ideas we don't share or want to protect from other people's arguments, but we could equally well treat these ideas as conclusions to be argued. We can make our apparently subjective, nonarguable opinions into arguable ideas by the way we present them and the way we enable our readers to reach them for themselves. If we present our views as mere opinions, there is very little reason for others to adopt them unless they know us personally, but if we present them as ideas with the necessary accessories to make them work, then other people might well have reason to take them very seriously indeed.

How do writers present ideas or opinions so that readers will participate in reading as they would in a conversation? One way is to build into the writing some opposition. How would the idea be opposed? How would someone argue to a different conclusion? How might someone else see your point? Asking these questions as you write and answering them in your writing is a vital step in getting beyond the stage of "it's just my opinion."

ACTIVITY 3–2: PARAPHRASING REVISITED

This activity invites you to learn how ideas come from interaction. We have already tried something like this with the "Star-Spangled Banner." In this activity, we will begin by paraphrasing the Pledge of Allegiance.

Preparation

More than twenty years ago, when the Supreme Court banned mandatory prayer in public schools, many more classrooms began having a daily Pledge of Allegiance to the Flag. You might not have spent whole days of your life reciting it, but you undoubtedly know it pretty well. Write it down, paraphrase it, and then pursue some ideas about it by answering these questions in notes. They are meant to help you find out the kinds of meaning that the Pledge has.

1. What is the basic act you perform in saying the Pledge? Of course you put your hand over your heart, but what do you accomplish by doing that? Do you perform acts like this anywhere else in your life?
2. Think back to the time when you first learned the Pledge. What did it mean to you then? Did you ever think about why the class began its day with such an event rather than, say, ending with it?
3. Has the Pledge meant anything different to you on any occasion? Would its appearance in a television movie surprise you? How would it have to be presented to be meaningful there?
4. Select several of the words of the Pledge for closer inspection. Perhaps you will choose "with liberty and justice for all." What experiences have you had that could explain the words "liberty" and "justice"? In your experience, does "liberty" mean freedom to do exactly as you please without being told what to do by anyone? Does "justice" mean that everyone is treated with perfect fairness? Is this phrase meant to describe how things are or how things ought to be—and how do you know?

Discussion

Compare your answers to these questions with the answers of other people in your writing group or class. The first question asks what the act of pledging really means. For you, it might be an expression of loyalty, while for someone else, it might be a promise; for another person, it might be a solemn oath. To what do you think the Pledge commits you? Does that agree with what other people think? Do many people think that the Pledge requires you to give up your life for your country if asked to do so? And yet small children are saying the Pledge before they understand the words— what does this mean to your group? Does the Pledge's statement that "liberty and justice" are available to all only express the hope that *someday* we will have liberty and justice for all?

Writing

This activity allows you to take account of the opinions of others in the formation of your own ideas. It allows you to move beyond simply expressing yourself on paper and to begin seriously to take account of other people. This works for many subjects, not just the Pledge, and is an important step toward considering the opinions of your readers as you write.

Now write out what the Pledge means to you and your group.

If you do not wish to use the Pledge, you might investigate something else that you all know "by heart." It might be an oath, a prayer, a song, a poem, a sales pitch, or something else. Write it down, paraphrase it, and examine it in the same sort of way: What exactly is its purpose? What does it do? What is it like? How and when did you learn it? What did it mean to you then, and what does it come to mean to you as you work with it? Why does it seem important or interesting? Discuss it with someone else. Finally, write out a joint account of what the piece means to all of you.

STRUCTURE

When we speak of the *structure* of a piece of writing, we are using a *metaphor*. That is, we are comparing something mysterious and difficult to talk about—writing—with something easier to talk about—something physical, like a building. It is, in short, a helpful way of talking about written words as if they were something else.

The structural metaphor allows us to talk about several related aspects of writing: What are the parts of a piece of writing? What job does each part do? How does each do its job? How are the parts related? The structural metaphor gives these questions and their answers a shape, a two- or three-dimensional picture, as if we were using a diagram, a flowchart, or some other visual representation. The metaphor provides words of physical space to describe the effects of lines or words that occur in time as a reader reads.

Many of the structures we find in expository prose are in fact guides for readers. A structure guides a reader by giving a shape, a map, a plan, before the reader has read very far. With a plan in mind, a reader can easily manage the material that follows, even if there is quite a lot of it, by filing it away in the right place, so to speak. This effect is particularly pronounced if the structure includes familiar patterns like giving causes for an effect, giving reasons for an opinion, telling a story with a point, anticipating likely objections to an argument, and comparing or contrasting two comparable things. But an individual structure can also be created for a particular piece of writing. (This is one of the skills developed by training in literature.)

Whether it is familiar or not, an effective structure allows readers to "place" the material they are receiving. Or we could say that structures function as the "organs" in organization; they are the ingredients of the writing that make it all work. Structures also help with sequence: they tell readers (and writers) what comes next, what has just finished, where they are in the whole picture, and where the whole enterprise is headed.

ACTIVITY 3–3: ANOTHER USE OF THE ANTHOLOGY

Preparation

For this activity, choose one of your contributions to the anthology from Activity 2–3 in the previous chapter, review its purpose and identify its overall plan: *how* is its purpose achieved through its various sections?

For example, one of the purposes of a scientific report is to make the results of an experiment as easily accessible to other researchers as possible, so most scientific reports begin with an abstract, a highly condensed summary of the results of the experiment described in the report. This summary abstract comes first so that readers in a hurry can decide if they need to read more of the report. It is not one of the purposes of such a report to create suspense by delaying the results until late in the report. Thus the section of the scientific report called the abstract serves the primary purpose of the report.

In showing how the plan of your selection works, you might want to consider these questions:

1. Does the order of the parts make special sense, or would other orders do equally well? A scientific report, for example, generally concludes with suggestions for further research, which would carry little weight unless we know what the report itself has established and by what methods, and so we could argue that this section must come last.

2. How is each part related to the adjacent parts? In a scientific report, the second section is usually "background"—previous research—and the next section is usually the formulation of the research problem and methods. The background section might show how the previous research provides both the terms and the logic for the procedures described in the methodology section, and, conversely, the methodology section might show how the current experiment differs from previous ones described in the background section (although in special cases an experimenter seeks to repeat exactly an experiment someone has already done).

3. Can you draw a visual equivalent for the structure of the writing as you see it?

Discussion

Compare your results with as many others as possible. Which structures have a great deal in common? Which seem totally opposite in strategy? Business reports, for example, will often have an abstract or summary of recommendations at the beginning so busy executives can get the conclusions first and examine the underpinnings later if needed, so they are like scientific reports in this way. But there are differences as well.

Writing

Summarize in a few paragraphs what you have learned about structure in expository prose. What are the important indicators of structure? What does structure accomplish? How does a writer know how to structure a piece of writing? (More questions might also be raised in your group's discussion.)

THE WRITER AND THE READER IN COLLABORATION

We will look more at structure in Chapter Five. Before continuing, however, let us examine how structure helps a writer effectively convey information, opinions, insights, or arguments to a group of active readers. Readers seem free to do almost as they please; how can they be made to do what a writer wants? The answer, of course, is that they can't.

Writers must settle for much less than compulsion. If readers behave as we have said they behave in Chapter Two, writers must see their task as much less directive than we might otherwise have thought. Readers can be invited, encouraged, guided by indications of purpose, provided with useful and interesting material in familiar structures—but they cannot be forced to interpret our writings as we might want. Even the most familiar of formats can't do that. Readers make their own meanings; writers can only suggest directions.

It might be easier if we could know for certain that a particular form was always going to be read in a particular way. There would always be an introduction, say, and the introduction would always be taken as a kind of road map for the terrain ahead. Perhaps it would always contain the point of the essay in a single sentence, and perhaps that point would always contain three subpoints; these would always be taken as the central message of the whole essay. Next, perhaps, there would be a "body" section. The body would always deliver exactly and directly on the three elements of the divided thesis statement by supplying evidence and reasons. Finally, there would always be a separate conclusion that would always be taken as a restatement of the main point.

Sometimes the format described in the previous paragraph—sometimes called the "five-paragraph theme"—is just what is needed, so it's not a bad trick to know, for instance to use on essay exams. But sometimes it is exactly the wrong thing to do. It offends some readers or seems too repetitive ("tell 'em what you're going to tell 'em, tell 'em, then tell 'em what you've told 'em") or too mechanical. Then it does the opposite of what the writer intends. A reader who is looking for a detailed analysis of causes or effects might find such a format distracting or too restrictive to allow the inclusion of necessary explanatory or supportive materials. If a general audience is going to read the writing, a more flexible form of organization might work better. In other words, the main thing that writers need to learn about structure is that it must be adapted to the needs of the audience.

If we are right about readers, they differ widely in their purposes for reading, in their methods of reading, in the experiences they supply to help themselves understand what the writer is saying, and in the groups in which we are going to encounter them, so that we must somehow allow for wide variations in what they will do. Writing for several people, each of whom will read your writing differently, is one of the hardest kinds of mental work. Not only will no single structure work reliably all the time, but neither will any particular style, tone, or strategy. Nothing we put into our writing can be guaranteed. This is a very painful conclusion to draw. It means that learning to write is not merely a matter of learning ways of doing things on a page. It is a matter of learning how to *negotiate* with readers about what is going to be on the page. And how can you negotiate with someone who isn't there while you are writing?

We will try some answers to that question shortly. But, however we answer it, we have at least advanced far enough to see that writers need to work in collaboration with readers rather than in competition with them. Writers must take as their limits the limits of their audience, must adjust their purposes to the purposes their readers can accommodate, must give readers familiar shapes for the new material to fit into, must allow readers to make of the text what readers' motives and past experiences seem to indicate. As writers, we can seek to achieve things that our readers will allow us to achieve, but to seek more would be like trying to lift ourselves by our own bootstraps—we would get in our own way.

If your reader is a partner in a common enterprise, or if you want to make it possible for the reader to be a partner, you must move some distance toward accommodating your partner's goals and purposes, and you must clearly indicate your own. You cannot expect to dominate such a collaborator, to tell him or her what to do. Nor do you allow the reader to dictate everything. Somehow you must find common ground from which to start, in ideas, in purposes, in structure; somehow too you must find agreed-on procedures by which to move ahead.

There are also ethical considerations in such a situation that would not arise if writing were simply a matter of putting words on a page. We have said that we cannot expect to manipulate our readers, because as readers we do not knowingly allow ourselves to be manipulated. Nor can we expect to swindle our readers. Readers, as many writers have said, must be treated with respect. If they aren't, if they become wary and suspicious, or, worse, if they sense intentions that they cannot accept, they will stop reading. Readers can and will do only the things we can and will do. There is a kind of Golden Rule here for writers to remember: Write as you would be written to.

So writers must negotiate with their readers and make allowances for the differences between them. They must think of their writing as a kind of invitation, an offering, a presentation of materials with guidelines for their examination, a suggestion of insight that does not preach and that places the reader on the same level as the writer. The reader must feel that there is room for him or her to work, helpful suggestions for how to do that work, and a clear indication of the writer's intentions regarding the work to be done.

This collaborative view of readers and writers helps to explain why it is so important to writers to get many people to respond to what they write. If you don't know the kinds of things readers are likely to do, you will end up frustrating or boring them. If you don't know what a reader is going to do with a particular section of your writing, you haven't yet made sure that the writing is going to work.

As you progress in a career, you must often adapt to new audiences, and this amounts to learning to write all over again, because you must learn to use new materials in new ways to get the new effects you want. Discouraging? Not if you know how you like to learn things. And not if you're willing to work closely *with* your new audience. What readers know, believe, and intend has everything to do with what they think good writing is. *Some* kind of writing will work for almost anyone, if you can find out what it is. Unfortunately, there are at last no certainties in writing, no guarantees, and no perfect or universal strategies. Nothing is going to work for everyone.

In the complicated matter of learning about audiences and strategies for writing, a freshman English class serves as a useful model for much of college or university experience. Freshmen often enter their post-secondary years expecting to acquire new information simply to fill in gaps in the information they already have. But college modifies even more commonly in other ways. Students find that the truth is far more complex than they had supposed. How you deal with complexity and uncertainty determines your success in college far more than how you deal with new information.

A FIRST LOOK AT CONVENTIONS

We have said that readers and writers must agree on how they are to proceed, must share some common ground so that they can understand one another. What are the areas of agreement?

Some of them involve the most basic mechanical aspects of writing—how letters are made, how words are spelled, how groups of words are punctuated, how certain grammatical functions must appear in all sentences. Some of these aspects are covered in Part Four.

Other conventions work at a level we might call structural—in such elements as paragraphs, for instance, which we will look at soon. Still others apply at the highest level of ideas and values, and it is a lifetime's work to try to understand what other people's ideas and values are. Some fairly simple agreements can relate ideas with structures, however, and those are the subject of the remainder of this chapter.

ACTIVITY 3–4: READING STRUCTURE FOR IDEAS

A more variable dimension of structure than we have discussed so far is *presentation*. If you look at a piece of writing as a whole, what are the proportions among the parts? Can you infer the importance of a section from its size? Or is its place in the sequence of parts a better guide to its importance?

Example

In a scientific report, the placement of the results (first, in the abstract) tells the reader that this is the most important element. On the other hand, the size of an editorial often indicates the importance that a newspaper attaches to the topic, and the size of individual paragraphs usually indicates as much about their importance as does their place in sequence.

Procedure

Examine another selection from your anthology, preferably one that you are not familiar with, so that you can see it with a fresh eye. What are its largest parts? Are they most important? What comes first and what last? Are these equally important, or does one dominate? What does the author seem to want to argue, based on the proportions of the various elements?

Repetition also plays a part in how a piece of writing is presented. Do you see indications that repetition is used in this selection? If it is used, what does it seem to mean? Is the repetition a matter of words, of ideas, or of something else?

Writing

Summarize the results of your inquiry into proportion and repetition and conclude by showing writers how to take advantage of this aspect of structure.

A FINAL NOTE:
MAKING NEW MATERIAL FAMILIAR

Writers make new material seem familiar. If the material seems too new, readers will miss it; if it seems too familiar, they will ignore it. Writers avoid both overfamiliarity and unnecessary novelty by balancing, structuring, shaping, and, above all, using good judgment. This good judgment comes from working with other people on writing, by seeing what works and what doesn't, by carefully observing other people's response to our words. We mature as writers through other people.

CHAPTER 4

How People Write—
The Processes

THE POINT OF THIS CHAPTER

This chapter provides information and suggestions to increase your familiarity with a variety of writing processes. It brings together the approaches to learning, reading, and writing from previous chapters. These materials should help you design some writing processes that suit you. The concluding activity of this chapter (Activity 4–5) asks you to *draft* a complete essay, even though your instructor might or might not want to assign an essay at this point in your course. Even if it is not required, such an assignment brings together all the concerns of this chapter.

PATTERNS OF LANGUAGE LEARNING

In observing adults as they learn, modern researchers have identified a pattern different from children's learning patterns. They find that adults progress through four stages:

1. Seeing alternatives to existing methods or knowledge

2. Trying one of these alternatives

3. Comparing alternatives on the basis of experience to see how the choice might be improved

4. Choosing principles by which to make that choice

This pattern shows a central fact about adult language learning, whether of a whole new language like French or Quechua or Japanese, or some new language habit within a known language, such as writing with more clarity or simplicity. The central fact about adult language learning is that it is almost always much more self-aware and self-directed than the language learning of children. Adults learn more deliberately and have greater control of their own learning.

The first step in improving one's writing, then, is to see what alternatives are available. That is not quite as easy as it sounds, apparently because successful learning depends on taking these alternatives seriously—something adults are not always willing to do. When we have already established patterns in any area of life, we have trouble visualizing alternatives and even more trouble imagining that they could work as well as what we already do.

A simple example is our regular way of greeting people. Perhaps we have a range of greetings: "Hi" and "How ya doin' " and "What's new?" Then we hear some new more formal greetings in a new situation, say a new job, like "Good morning" or "How are you?" We are unlikely to change until we perceive that the new forms of greeting are accepted by other people in that job and until we recognize that our usual ways of saying hello are a bit odd for others, a bit jarring or distracting, so that we begin to see that change would be a good idea. At that point, we can seriously consider adding some of these new greetings to our stock.

A similar sequence of events must occur before we can change our writing habits. We must see that our current habits aren't working as well as they might and that some people around us have writing habits that work better. At this point, we can take a genuine interest in changing our ways of writing, because we have a reason to do so and at least a few alternatives from which to choose.

ACTIVITY 4–1: CLICHÉS

Purpose

In making your writing more effective, you will want to avoid words, phrases, or sentences that are too predictable. In a conversation, you wouldn't tell your friends something they already know. They would be bored, maybe even insulted, at the hint that they were forgetful or inexperienced or ignorant. Similarly, readers expect writers to "make it new."

You won't know what's new to a general audience until you've had some experience, but you can begin by avoiding the overly simple, overly general, overly familiar words, phrases, and sentences that are almost "automatic language" for most of us.

Generations ago, many of these expressions were colorful. "Haste makes waste" had a nice rhyme, and rhyme can be a powerful aid to memory. We can feel a similar effect in the more recent "No pain, no gain." This activity is meant to help you become aware of such familiar language so that you can avoid it or rework it into something new that you can then use effectively.

Procedure

Begin by collecting five familiar phrases or sentences that you actually hear. You probably won't hear "cute as a bug's ear," but you might hear "What goes around comes around" or "Don't make waves" or "Dress for success." Some phrases become so common they are almost unnoticed: "the right stuff," "cut so-and-so down to size," "the last straw." Others stand out: "the shop-till-you-drop capital" of a county or large area, "the best thing since sliced bread."

In a group of three or four, construct a story using everyone's collections of clichés. When you read the story to other groups, see if they notice all the items you have included. As you read your story, you will be helping other people learn to listen for these worn-out expressions.

The second step in working with clichés is to notice that, for every cliché that gives advice, there is another that gives exactly the opposite advice. So there's a cliché to back up almost whatever you want to do. For example, if you are wondering whether to do something you must do now or not at all, you might remember either "He who hesitates is lost" or "Look before you leap," "Opportunity knocks but once" or "Don't buy a pig in a poke." (It's interesting that many of these expressions preserve words that are no longer in general use, like "poke" as a noun meaning "sack.")

Find as many pairs of contradictory clichés as you can, beginning with these:

Two heads are better than one, *but* too many cooks spoil the broth.

What's sauce for the goose is sauce for the gander, *but* different strokes for different folks.

Keep your nose to the grindstone, *but* stop to smell the flowers.

Can you find opposites for the following?

When the going gets tough, the tough get going.

You get what you pay for.

Never look a gift horse in the mouth.

Don't count your chickens before they hatch.

Don't put all your eggs in one basket.

Can you find other pairs?

Once you have collected these paired clichés, you are ready to try making some of your clichés new. Many jokes are made this way, by putting a surprising ending onto a predictable cliché— "Never put off until tomorrow what you can avoid completely"—or by building a story around plays on words in a cliché—"People who live in grass houses shouldn't stow thrones." Choose a cliché and try to turn it inside out in some way.

Reflection

The last step in this process goes beyond this book and beyond most of our skills. Some of the best writers have a knack for inventing phrases or sentences that seem familiar even though they are new, that seem inevitable even though they are creations of someone's point of view.

A writer famous for such phrases—called *epigrams*—is Oscar Wilde who was often content to use them just for wit. For example, he speaks of a woman whose husband died and whose hair as a result "went quite gold with grief," meaning that she took what should have been a sad occasion as a chance to dye her hair. Other writers have used them to make profound observations. Dickens said of the French Revolution, "It was the best of times, it was the worst of times . . .," and Tolstoy wrote, "All happy families are happy in the same way, but each unhappy family is unhappy in its own way."

Even if literature is not part of your writing course, however, you can still take advantage of the insights it offers. Readers like memorable phrases, balanced sentences, and wit because they make reading easier and more fun. If you can find such short, punchy ways to state points—not too often, probably, or the effect is diminished—you will add extra impact to your writing.

MOTIVATION FOR CHANGE

Television and movies often show writers as very special people. Sometimes they show writers as gifted and sensitive, people who simply look inside and then write down the very special meanings they find there. Or perhaps they show writers as aggressive and inquisitive, with a sure instinct for truth and an exact knowledge of how to put that truth down. We tend to give such people the status of Writer with a capital letter. Consequently we may think that we could never be writers at all.

But we *are* writers, at least with a small letter. We write lists, letters, notes about things we must do tomorrow, memos, complaints, requests, journals or diaries, and many other things. In all our writings, even though we may not feel that they are worth noticing *as writing*, we are doing what even the greatest Writers do—we are shaping, organizing, and influencing our experience or behavior. It is important that we recognize how we already behave as writers because we will build on these familiar writing processes by improving them and adding to them.

ACTIVITY 4–2: WHAT KIND OF WRITER ARE YOU?

Do you make lists? Do you write letters? Do you ever make notes to yourself about tomorrow or next week? Do you write notes or memos to other people? Do you keep some kind of daily log, a record of your reading or reflections or activities? Do you write things down about your parents, grandparents, or ancestors, or about the first few months of a new baby in your family? If you do, you have personal experience with some of the things writers do: making sense of confusion, recording something, planning, persuading, recommending.

Write a description of yourself as a writer, using enough

examples to show other people what *sort* of note writer or list maker you are.

For example, do you use a list as an organizing tool and then leave it, or do you mark off things as they are done? Do your letters flow as your mind flows, or do they usually have a more specific purpose? What kinds of writing have you done for jobs? And did you like it? Most important of all, how would you connect your view of your writing with your personality? One writer I know describes himself this way: "I am a gol-danged knobby-kneed awkward stumbling wrestling stubborn sort of writer."

Another important dimension to consider in assessing yourself as a writer is the way you prefer to write. For example, the set of steps or sequence of things you do is called your writing process: When you have something long to write, such as a paper for school, what process do you follow? What do you do first, second, third? Also, where do you prefer to write? At what time of day? Have you ever written something in cooperation with other people? If so, what was your reaction to the experience? Put down whatever you know of your writing habits and preferences.

The point of describing what kind of writer you are at this point is to help you see where you might go from here. So consider next the areas in which you would like to improve. You might have some difficulties with mechanical aspects of writing, with spelling, for instance. Perhaps you feel that improving your spelling should have a high priority, or perhaps you feel that spelling can wait while you improve your ability to organize or to generate ideas. Maybe a good goal for you at this point is simply to use writing in new and different ways. This activity invites you to reflect on some of your goals as an improving writer.

THE RANGE OF ALTERNATIVES

Think about a writer at work. The picture most of us have in our heads corresponds in many details to the popular myth about the good reader presented in Chapter Two. For one thing, "good readers" are supposed to be fast, and we may think that good writers are fast too. Second, just as "good readers," are supposed to take in material easily and without resistance, so we may think that good writers know by instinct how to arrange material so that others can take it in easily or have some prepared formats or other techniques for ensuring that their material is easily absorbed.

Third, if we think that "good readers" retain material almost word for word, we might suppose that good writers naturally phrase things in the most memorable ways. And of course we are likely to believe that good writers are never at a loss for what to write.

The truth is that these "good writers" can be found where the "good readers" are—in Never-Never Land. All the abilities of good writers are normally the result of effort not natural gifts. Many successful writers are very slow; Pulitzer Prize–winner Donald Murray has confessed to being amazed at how rapidly many student writers compose. Interviews with professional writers also show that most spend lots of time working over their arrangement, trying different orders for their material and different links between sections, adding and subtracting examples, and so on. The idea that good writers have a natural ability to phrase things in the best way is also wrong; that phrase that sounds just right might have taken the writer days to develop through thirty different versions.

Most striking of all, many professional writers are just as bothered by new assignments or tasks as the rest of us and worry about "running dry" even more since their livelihood depends on a flow of ideas. Many people don't like admitting to feelings of fear or inadequacy, but the truth for almost all of us is exactly what a student wrote for an activity like the previous one: The first thing that comes into her mind when facing a writing assignment is terror. She feels inadequate. She thinks about dropping the course. She can't think up a new topic and can't think of anything to say about an assigned one. She is sure her teacher will think she is stupid. She has no idea what she should do first, or second, or ever, to find a manageable topic, to find information, to argue for her opinion.

It is often a relief to nonprofessionals to hear that professional writers talk about the same feelings at the beginning of a writing task: too little time, not enough knowledge, feelings of inadequacy and fears of exposure, a desire to avoid the whole thing, an urge to sharpen pencils or straighten the house or keep busy so as to avoid thinking (at least consciously) about what is to come.

What we do with these feelings partly determines the kinds of writers we are. Some people need to rely on a procedure. Others need to stay flexible, perhaps going at the writing a bit differently every time. Some immediately lay out a plan for writing, a little each day, while others put everything off as long as possible. Many of us seem to feel that we *should* start right away and feel guilty when we don't.

In talking with people about how they write, I have found several types of procrastination. One kind results from that unrealistic picture of how "good writers" write. "I can't start because I don't know enough," some people will say. But nobody writes everything correctly the first time, and it is often helpful for such people to begin by writing down specifically what they do already know about their topic even if they think it's not enough, because writing down what you know can often suggest first that you know more than you thought and second that you have some particular interest in pursuing the topic.

Another kind of procrastination actually helps the writers who practice it. These writers will say things like this:

> I read over the assignment (or I think about the topic or I imagine the committee reading our report, or whatever) several times until I practically have it by heart. I think about what a good answer would be like. Then I absolutely refuse to think about the whole project at all for a few days because that is "cooking" time for my subconscious (or unconscious) mind. Finally, when I feel all charged up with material or thoughts, or when the adrenaline from the approaching deadline hits, I burn the words out.

So important is this habit to some writers that it has received a name: the Law of Delay. The Law of Delay says that at some time in your writing process a little delay will add greatly to the quality of what you write.

Besides giving your unconscious mind the opportunity to assist in your writing, the delay approach also allows you to write under the influence of a strong emotion, another trick of professional writers. Perhaps you have noticed that writing a complaint when you are angry seems to make you more fluent; the words come easier. (Revising may be a different story, of course.) According to the Law of Delay, you should wait for that emotion if you are someone who likes the extra intensity.

The Law of Delay is an alternative for the person who feels terror at the thought of writing. In just the same way, there are alternatives ways of coping with, even taking advantage of, the difficulties any of us face throughout the writing process. Things may seem discouraging at first, even overwhelming. Writing isn't easy even for the pros, and that can make us feel that writing will always be even harder for us. On the other hand, we should recognize that good writers start where we start. Perhaps we can learn from them.

ACTIVITY 4–3: HOW WRITERS WRITE

The library is full of accounts of how people write. Working from a shared list of writers given by your instructor, assign each member of your group a single writer to investigate and report on. Find an article or book in the library that shows how your writer composed. Perhaps you can find personal reminiscences or an interview or even some discussion by critics of existing drafts.

When you report to your group and listen to the other reports, try to classify the writers by strategies. Listen to the second report for similarities to and differences from the first; see whether the third is more like the first or the second.

CHOOSING A METHOD TO TRY

An entire writing program could be developed just from reports of what professional writers do. The program would, however, contradict itself frequently.

Consider *outlining*, for example. Some writers outline sketchily in the early phase of the writing process, giving only a note or two to indicate each part of a whole. A writer composing a personal essay about the meaning of several of the important places of her childhood might use a note about each place:

A. My closet—place for fantasy
B. My room—place for display of objects
C. My spot downstairs—for listening
D. My tree—for watching without being seen
E. My fort—games

Even if she is further along, she may well settle for a note about the details and significance of each place; "my closet—where I kept my books and toys, especially the ones I used in my fantasy-games" and "I have continued to keep a place and role for fantasy in my life now." She may settle for an A, B, C, . . . with a few words after each because she is using the outline simply to keep herself on track. The outline reminds and guides but does not control the writing.

Others may do detailed outlines, showing the divisions of a whole into A, B, C, and so on and then the divisions of each of these into two or more parts, in great detail, and giving each entry a whole sentence. Such an outline might begin like this:

Point: These places shaped the adult I am now
  A. closet
    1. fantasy games
      a. then: I used to imagine myself as the heroine of stories I'd read, Heidi and Guenevere and Eloise
      b. now: I still project myself into what I read, Eudora Welty or Alice Walker or Margaret Atwood
    2. clothes
      a. then: I had plenty of clothes, and I liked to wear as many as I could before wearing the same thing again
      b. now: still do the same
    3. books and toys
      a. then: Each book and toy had its own special place, and I was a perfectionist about neatness
      b. now: I still keep some toys around—lots of books—all with their special places
  B. My room
    1. bed
      a. then: I had a huge colorful afghan my grandmother had made
      b. now: I spread out a large antique quilt

This writer uses the outline not only to generate material but also to control the flow of it during the first (or zero) draft. Because the *use* of the outline is different, the outline itself looks different. It allows a writer to organize *before* drafting.

There are other writers who outline much later, *after* a draft or even two, inserting numbers and letters into the text to help them discover what the real organization of their thought has been so that they can make that arrangement more obvious to a reader. In doing a draft, for instance, a writer might discover (rather than decide beforehand) that she was very interested in the contrast of then and now, in how she has evolved from the child who chose different places for different moods. She devises a two-part structure, the first very like what is described in the outlines above but without the "now" and the second a single paragraph that collects her thoughts about the spaces she uses now, perhaps centering around the idea that her life isn't as rich as it used to be, since her places are reduced to only a few whose functions are dictated by job, family, and friends or roommates.

The point is that outlines or any writing strategy will change to suit the function you give it in your writing process; it is far more important to consider the function than to worry about satisfying the requirements of any given strategy. Consider revision, for another example. Some writers revise as they write, getting every word right before going on, while others rush through to complete a draft, then go back and revise the whole. In the first case, revision is closely tied to the generative process, and as a result it looks like a word-by-word affair. This is in fact how many less skilled writers revise because they think revision is just a matter of getting the right word choice. They don't realize that it also includes point of view, tone, structure, examples or other support, and many other things. But even skilled writers may revise that way, as magazine writers often say they do once they have memorized the particular structure and tone that a particular magazine editor wants from them. Other writers need to see the whole before they know how to fix the parts, and so they wait to make changes until they have a clear idea about the overall direction of what they are writing. Revision for these writers is a distinct step, and it allows them to focus on a few specific questions, such as whether they have supplied enough support, whether their argument really holds, and so on. (Later in the book we will return several times to the important topic of revision.)

The same point fits all writing activities. No two writers seem to do things the same way, and generalizations about what the behavior of writers as a group look pretty shaky as a result. How can this be? Aren't there regularities in the ways all writers work? Can't we find out what the best tricks are? Can't we at least isolate two or three methods to which most writers approximate? And anyway, these reports from professional writers don't say much about how students should write, do they?

The best way to answer these questions, I think, is to realize that, even if some generalizations fit most writers, they will be so general that each of us will have to work out the details for ourselves. Writers differ, perhaps even more than readers do. Many writers seem to have worked as hard at designing their methods of writing as they have at writing any particular work. They have found out how to surround themselves with just the right conditions, just the right distractions and rewards; they know what pace is right. They know what makes writing important for them, and they know what satisfactions it offers. In all these ways, they have individualized their writing, and their example is worth imitating.

To begin with, most writers can identify stages in their writing processes. There are preliminary activities, maybe with doodling or brainstorming or other generative aids but maybe with nothing visible except sitting and staring out the window or off into space, or even giving oneself a problem and then going to sleep and letting some nonconscious part of the brain take over. These activities are often called *prewriting* or "rehearsal" because they come ahead of seriously trying out a draft, even though they lead to such a draft. Some people don't even need preliminary activities, of course, but move right to the next stage.

In the stage generally called *composing* or *drafting* or just plain writing, people begin to put on paper the thoughts and expressions they think have some chance of ending up in a finished product. Some people like to write a "zero draft," a strictly private sketching of material; others like to go immediately to a first draft in which they can work out as much of the idea and structure of the final version as possible. On essay exams, people often find that this draft must be the final copy, so they also try to get the mechanics of writing correct at the same time.

After composing, many people allow a break in their writing process, an interval during which nothing much happens except that time passes. A few days is usually enough to give most people a look at their own writing "from the outside," so to speak—as if they were readers and not the writers. Seeing your writing as others will see it is important because it helps you make your meaning much more obvious. You can tell where the gaps are, where the examples don't show quite what you wanted, where the words sound a little peculiar. This is the point at which many writers get others to read and comment also—before revising. Some people like lots of readers; some like only one. At any rate, the last stage of writing involves revising—literally, re-seeing—and then editing and proofreading, making sure the structure and mechanics of the writing are in order.

These stages are approximate, of course. Any writer may avoid one or more, may spend a lot of time doing things in one or another of these stages. They are not rules, and they aren't guarantees either. They are simply suggestions based on how some other writers write.

What is most noticeable about reports on professional writers is not so much that they include these three stages of prewriting, writing, and rewriting but that they show very different activities for each of the stages. The outlining mentioned before is only one example; almost any activity can figure in prewriting, writing, or rewriting. In the following activities, you will find procedures that you are encouraged to use at the right moment in your own writing, a moment only you can determine.

ACTIVITY 4–4: FREEWRITING

Many writers have some kind of brainstorming or loosening exercise they use to get going or to get ideas. An especially common one is called *freewriting*. It is not quite "free," because there is one iron rule: the writing implement must keep moving for the time allotted, usually ten minutes.

Freewriting is not graded. Usually it is not even collected by a teacher. The point of it is not so much what you have left when you finish, but what you do during the time allotted. You set aside all thoughts of spelling, punctuation, capitalization, and good grammar, even of sentences. You put down as fast as you can what is actually going through your mind.

Procedure

The first time you try freewriting, you should have no topic. (Later your teacher might suggest one, but most writers work better in the freewriting and get more out of it if they select its directions for themselves—see the suggested uses of freewriting listed below.) Just keep writing "today is tuesday today is tuesday today is tuesday" if you like, or put down a thought that comes to you and then go back to repeating a single word or two until another thought comes. The first objective of freewriting is accomplished in just this way: it increases most people's "fluency," their ability simply to get words on the page faster. Even if you never use freewriting for anything else, you can help yourself by using it for this, because it will enable you to get more on paper during essay tests. Like any physical exercise, the physical act of writing is one that can be speeded up with practice.

Pick an amount of time during which you will freewrite. Most people use eight, ten, or twelve minutes. Choose a good time— early morning, late at night, on the bus. Try freewriting every day for at least five days to give yourself a chance to get comfortable with its one rule.

Reflection

By the second or third time you try freewriting, you might begin to notice that you have improved your ability to write down your thoughts. This is the second objective of freewriting, and for most people it happens automatically. An improved connection between head and hand is one way of describing the result. If you are able to make progress in writing down your thoughts, you might want to think about keeping the papers you freewrite since they might have ideas in them you would like to pursue. But many writers simply throw away their freewritings, treating them exactly like workouts.

Suggestions

If you get comfortable with the physical activity of freewriting and have begun to be able to put your thoughts down, you might like to try to "push." Some writers are able to keep the pen or pencil ahead of their conscious minds, just a little. Doing so takes advantage of the idea behind freewriting, that you can improve your writing by separating it into a generative part and a critical part. Freewriting is obviously the generative part; it can tell you what you really think about a idea, why you really care about it, or how you can show it vividly to someone else. Some people use it to tell the unpleasant truths they later modify in their drafts, and find that saying things straight out in this way helps them clarify their real intentions. "I'd like to tell those guys to get off the steroids, but I know they are just the ones who won't listen," a student wrote recently in one of my classes. Then he was able to decide on an audience he could write to, an audience of athletes who haven't yet made up their minds about using steroids, and he gave up trying to preach to people who already use them. But freewriting carries no guarantee, of course; some days you come up empty. For some people, also, it doesn't help.

Freewriting can help some writers in drafting or revising. It can help them get "unstuck," particularly if they prompt themselves by saying, "Well, what's so stuck about this topic right here? What's the difficulty?" "Maybe there's really *nothing* we can do about pollution," a student recently wrote, and she was able to see why her project on stopping air pollution was becoming so difficult. Because there is no pressure to make freewriting actually do anything in the finished product, writers find that it helps them see around their difficulties. That writer went on to recast her paper, and included her own assessment of the futility of existing air quality controls. The paper changed and that made more work, to be sure, but it was work she cared about more than she did about the less appealing paper whose writer, as she put it, "pretended" that air quality could be improved.

Freewriting has many other uses as well. If you or your teacher poses a topic or a problem, you can use freewriting to explore what you already know without committing yourself to a position. You can use freewriting after a lecture to put down points that interested you; you can use it before a lecture to predict what will happen in a particular class. You can use it in the middle of a class to help you formulate a question or argument.

Just like freewriting and outlining, other activities can be effective at various points in the writing process. The fifty-specifics technique of Activity 2–2 was presented as a way of generating material prior to drafting, but it can also be used in revision when a writer decides that something absolutely essential is missing. Nobody likes your opening? A paragraph that began a student paper in a bland way came alive through this process; can you tell what some of the specifics were?

First draft: Sport touring on a motorcycle is where it's at. Sport touring is where you get a sport bike, pack up some gear, and take a trip. The main difference is that sport touring uses windy roads.

Second draft: This summer I plan on taking a tour of the West on my bike, no matter how sore my rear end gets. I'll camp out at night, picking the bugs out of my teeth. I'll need my KZ 400, some soft luggage, a waterbottle, and a map. I'll avoid things like guardrails, dead animals, and the endless miles of dreadfully straight pavement you see on freeways. . . .

CONCLUDING ACTIVITY: CONSTRUCTING YOUR OWN PROCESS

Procedure

You now have a variety of materials from which to begin designing your own writing process. You have read several other students' descriptions of themselves as writers, which probably included at least a few activities you hadn't heard of before. You have heard about the Law of Delay, about freewriting, about revising by the fifty-specifics technique. You have read about one professional author's techniques, and you have heard about a number of others'. For this activity, design your own process, from prewriting through drafting (we will work with revision later, in Chapter 12), and include in it at least one strategy you haven't used before.

This activity requires you to choose a subject and an audience as well as a point and a means of making that point. That is a lot to think about, but it is all part of the writer's job. You may be uncomfortable trying to do all this at first; many students are. But, after a trial or two, most people prefer this kind of freedom and come to feel that restrictive assignments are too confining.

Suggestions

You already have a list of activities to choose from, based on discussions of other people's writing processes. But here are some additional suggestions designed to help you find alternatives to your present habits.

In the prewriting stages, you might consider:

Freewriting
Keeping a journal or diary (See Chapter Five, pp. 82—83)
Brainstorming (jotting down notes rapidly by association)

Mapping (making any kind of map of ideas, a kind of two-dimensional brainstorming, using all the space around words to draw
connections with other words or ideas)

Conversation and discussion (finding topics that you have talked
about recently with friends that might be interesting to pursue
further)

Looking at pictures or listening to music

Reading or researching

Paraphrasing or summarizing (as in Chapter One), then extending
and applying something you have read

Identifying a common problem and proposing a solution

Interviewing someone by the fifty-specifics technique

In the drafting stages, you might consider:

Doing a "zero draft" or discovery draft (writing down for your own
eyes only what you are thinking about or what you already
know about a topic before researching it)

Generalizing (determining the largest significance of the topic)

Particularizing (deciding how much more specific you can be about
the topic)

Stating your purpose directly at the beginning; not stating your
purpose until the end; not stating your purpose directly at all

Supporting your point only with actual events that you witnessed or
participated in

Looking at your topic from someone else's point of view first; if you
want to argue something, arguing the opposition's side first

Addressing your writing to an unusual audience (the very young,
the very old, those from another culture or planet)

Trying to sound older or younger than you are

Reflection

Before showing a completed draft to others, try to determine
how all the change in tactics has worked for you. Did it get you to
write things you otherwise wouldn't have written? How effectively
did the new activity actually improve your writing?

A FINAL NOTE: FLEXIBILITY

Current research on writing shows that different people write differently. We have seen that such variety makes sense, given our differences in learning habits, in reading, in the way we see writing situations. What is surprising and challenging in the research is that competent writers seem to be the ones who continuously *adapt* their writing processes to changing circumstances.

In Chapter One, we talked about personalizing the advice other writers might give you. We can now say more concretely that good writers need to know about a wide variety of writing techniques that they can fit to each individual task. You need to know your best time of day for getting ideas, and you also need to know how to get some ideas at the bad times. You need to be able to edit by yourself and also take advantage of the comments other people make. You need to know how to write with maximum compression and also how to write at full length.

How do people write? The answer seems to be that they write best when they write flexibly, when they have many strategies to choose from, and when they have some experience in knowing which ones are more likely to work.

CHAPTER 5

How People Learn
to Write

THE POINT OF THIS CHAPTER

Is writing a skill, or more than a skill? The answer makes a great deal of difference to how we go about learning to write.

If writing were only a skill, we could expect to master it in a short time, once and for all. Like typing and driving a car, we would expect to spend a few months at it before mastering it, and we would expect to maintain our skill with occasional practice.

But many people who write see writing as a great deal more than just a skill. For one thing, it offers many people individual rewards that are suited to them and not available any other way. In proportion to these rewards, it is harder to learn, and in fact requires an approach different from those we would employ to learn skills.

In particular, learning to write requires a firm sense of *why* one is learning. In this chapter, we focus on the close connection between writing and learning. Many of the things people do with writing improve their learning, and almost any learning is improved by the use of writing in one way or another. People who write often say also that they are "always learning."

Another difference between learning to write and learning a skill is that writing requires other people. Unlike many physical skills, which require practice and coaching, writing seems to require practice, coaching, and—the responses of other people. It is as if one needed not only a coach but a stadium full of people to learn gymnastics or football.

Furthermore, writing requires considerable ability to examine our own thinking for flaws. In order to write so other people will read the result, we must learn to anticipate the ways readers will test and probe what we say. We take the opinions of other people as guides in learning to think critically about our own words.

Finally, we can learn to write only if we acknowledge that our learning is never complete. This last difference between learning to write and learning a skill is a bit mysterious, but, like the others, it follows from the real nature of writing.

WHAT WRITING IS REALLY LIKE

When you learn to ride a bicycle, someone helps you until you get the trick of it or the knack, and then you can ride. Even if you haven't ridden a bicycle for years, you still expect the knack to be there; you believe that you will know how to ride the next time you get on a bicycle.

There may be more advanced skills—cross-country bicycling, racing, working as a bicycle messenger—but they are simply additions to or refinements of the basic skill. There are also subskills, parts of the basic skill that can be learned separately, such as pedaling (which many children learn on tricycles), balancing, turning, braking, signaling, riding with no hands.

Writing seems to parallel skills like bicycling in a number of ways. We are supposed to learn basic writing skills at the beginning of our college careers that we can use in our later work, much as we learn basic bicycling skills before we attempt to enter races. The idea of "freshman writing" seems to suggest that there is a knack or trick that can be mastered once and for all. People talk about getting rusty in writing, needing a refresher, and so on, and they do so because they expect writing to come back to them the way riding a bicycle or swimming does.

We sometimes see that people who can write in one way seem to be able to use their ability to write in a variety of fields. This makes us think of writing as a single skill that can be applied to a variety of situations. It also makes us think of writing as a talent, something you are more or less born with or without, since some people seem to have this broad ability and some don't.

But this idea of writing as a skill doesn't fit all the facts. For one thing, the "fade" is too dramatic. Research over the last quarter century has shown that, despite intensive writing courses, college students don't maintain their ability to write unless they keep writing. This effect wouldn't exist if writing were a knack like swimming or riding a bicycle.

Recent research has also disproved the notion that writing has subskills. Instruction in grammar doesn't improve writing; neither does instruction in spelling. The research has suggested that we should think about writing as we think about molecules: we don't expect water to behave like either hydrogen or oxygen or even like a mixture of the two, although we know it is made out of them, because the water molecule is a distinct substance, one that can't be taken apart without destroying it and replacing it with substances very different from it. The same point applies to writing: If we take it apart, we get subskills that aren't very much like writing at all. So we say nowadays that we learn to write by writing, not by learning subskills.

Is writing a universal skill? Can it be learned once and then applied to a variety of fields? The answer here is more complicated than "yes" or "no" because the ability to write does seem to carry over to some extent from one field to another, but the carry-over is far from complete. People who change jobs, for instance, and have to change the kind of writing they do, generally report a "period of adjustment" during which they learn their way around the new writing requirements.

Other research shows that, as people progress through their careers and encounter new challenges and obstacles, their old writing problems often reappear for a short while at the new level. This kind of information suggests that some aspect of writing might be universal—perhaps it is just the confidence that you *can* adjust to the new situation—but that the carry-over is more limited than we would expect if writing were really a talent.

So recent research indicates that, although writing might sometimes *look like* a skill, in fact there is more to it than that. Why do people have the needlessly limited "skill" view of writing then? One reason might be that people who do not write much find it hard to see what goes on when people write. They have no experience by which to judge the usual views of writing. Another reason may be simply habit. We have only recently replaced the skill view of writing with a better view, and it takes time to bring people up to date.

Another reason might be that people are often fooled by words. The particular kind of error involved has been studied by people working in the field of *general semantics*, who call it *reification*. The label means "making a thing" where no thing was before, and the error (which language encourages us to make) is to assume that, because we have a word for something, there must be a thing that the word refers to. "Writing" seems to refer to one thing, one skill, and so we "reify" the word and act as if one skill corresponded to the one word.

To defend ourselves against reification, we need to remember that writing is much more complicated than we usually think. But merely reminding ourselves is generally not enough. We need a better mental picture of writing.

DEVELOPING A BETTER VIEW

Deliberately trying to change the way we think about something is one of the hardest acts any adult can perform. If you ask people, many will say that they simply cannot do it. They know that their minds change, but the changes just seem to happen rather than to result from an act of will.

People who *are* able to change their minds report a couple of useful strategies. One strategy draws on memories of other people—you speak to yourself as if you were someone else, "Come on, you, look at what's really going on here," and you give yourself the new picture or advice or point of view that someone else might give. This technique is particularly useful in writing because it leads naturally to revision, as we will see. Another technique uses metaphors (see Chapter Three), which affect the pictorial part of our minds where our basic view of writing gets much of its strength.

In the metaphoric approach to changing your mind, you replace your picture of writing as a skill (like bike riding) with a new picture. Suppose writing a memo is like playing a game. Writing a letter is obviously a different game. Writing in a journal is a third game. Writing a report is a fourth, an essay a fifth, an essay test a sixth, an article a seventh, a press release an eighth. Learning to play one game isn't learning to play any other game, although there may be similarities and some degree of carry-over. Games are so different, in fact, that there probably couldn't be any theory of games (any general principles about writing) that would apply to all of them, although we can give some good advice about most games.

Or think of writing as knowing how to use tools or how to travel. When you learn to use tools, you don't learn general principles; you learn how to use this screwdriver to drive this screw into this kind of material. When you learn to use a saw, you get very little transfer from what you know about screwdrivers. Any particular job you want to tackle will require its own set of tools. A new tool might or might not be like the ones you already know, and the most we can say about learning the new one is that some confidence in yourself as a tool user is going to be a help. But, because tools are all so different, there really isn't one skill called "tool using," and so of course there also isn't much of a general theory of tool using to go by.

Similarly, the first time you travel somewhere, you have a destination, and some way of getting there, and things you want to do when you get there. The next time, you remember how things went, but now the destination is different; perhaps you will travel in a different means of transportation, and you will do different things when you get there. Eventually you become an experienced traveler, but still you have to rethink your traveling when you head for a new place by new means to do new things.

Playing games, using tools, and traveling are like writing. The fact that we have a single word for each shouldn't make us think that we are talking about a single skill. In fact, we are talking in each case about a quite complicated set of abilities, a set that might actually change from time to time or place to place.

Why do we need a more complete view of writing? In order to learn most effectively, we need an accurate picture of what we are learning. Which games are we going to learn first? What tools will we use on what job? Where and how are we going to travel, and what will we do when we get there? More important still, how will we prepare for the *next* kind of game, the next job and set of tools, the next trip? It is characteristic of adults to learn these things deliberately, with their eyes open, not memorizing as we often expect children to do, but consciously, intentionally, with full participation. These characteristics of adult learners also make it clear that we need a more complete view of writing if we are going to learn about it.

In the next activity, which focuses on the so-called "skill" of defining, you are invited to consider ways in which defining really goes beyond the boundaries of a "skill," and you are also invited to reflect on what this wider view of defining might mean about writing as a whole.

ACTIVITY 5–1: DEFINING

Purpose

A very basic writing task or job is defining. There are several types of definition, including functional, extended, and others. The kind you are asked to write here is definition by classification, in which you explain what something is by putting it into a larger class of similar items and then by distinguishing it from the other similar items.

The item to define is the "automatic language" that was the subject of several previous activities in this book. Examples include the "Star-Spangled Banner" (before paraphrasing), the Pledge of Allegiance (before you examined it carefully), clichés, and other examples you identified (for some people, these include prayers, oaths for clubs or organizations, nursery rhymes and lullabies, special vocabularies, slang, words to songs, and so on). You need not keep the term "automatic" if you decide that the item is really something else.

Procedure

To what general category do you assign the phenomenon of automatic language? Is it one kind of language use? To define it, then, you would separate it from other types of language use, most of which presumably aren't automatic. Is it better seen as one type of routine behavior? Then you will distinguish it from other kinds of routine behavior, probably by the ingredient of language. Or you might find some other category into which it fits.

How do you separate it from other members of the category? It would be too simple to divide all language use into automatic and nonautomatic, but that might be a place to start if you can say what "nonautomatic" uses of language are. Then perhaps you will see intermediate cases, or a third separate category that is neither automatic nor nonautomatic. But you might not want to start with a two-way split at all.

When you have written your definition, this activity is half done. The second half asks you to reflect on what you have done in defining.

Reflection

As we have mentioned before, adults reflect on their learning more than children do; they learn by assimilating rather than simply by absorbing or memorizing.

There is much to reflect on in this activity, although not all the questions that follow will be useful to you in guiding your reflection. Choose the ones that seem to suit your definition, and answer them in an attempt to become more aware of what writing is like for you. Some of the questions are hard because they ask how you know some of the things that you often just seem to know. These are the questions that people have found the most rewarding to wrestle with; it is as if finding out how you know things helps you see how the different things you know are connected.

In writing a definition, you did things that went beyond mere skills. You chose examples of the phenomenon and presumably excluded others. How did you do that? On what principle? By what right? Would the effect of choosing other examples have been a different definition or chaos? Would you say that choosing the examples was a subskill of defining? If not, what is its connection?

More important still, you located your chosen group of examples in relation to some other items. You chose to include, say, the National Anthem and the Pledge, but not prayers. Where did you get the information or skill to do that? Had you ever made a definition of some items of your experience before? What seems to you a reason for doing so, or a possible benefit of doing so? Is the definition any less immediate or complete than the experiences of the items you define? And, in general, what would you call this process of defining? Is it thought? Is it analysis? Is it intuition? Or what? Is there anything in this process that you think might be useful in some other kind of writing? Would you want to take on such a writing task some time?

WRITING AND LEARNING

When research into writing processes really got going less than twenty years ago, people began noticing almost at once that the early parts of these processes were very interesting. Because they were the generative parts of writing, they seemed to offer a good opportunity to study creativity. That research has resulted in the widespread use of activities like journalkeeping and freewriting. But these activities turned out to show another side of writing as well, one that might have even more important implications than the creative side. Writing, particularly the kind that occurs early in the process, can be an enormously powerful tool for learning.

This was a rather paradoxical turnabout of researchers' expectations. Looking for better ways of learning to write, they found ways of writing to learn. The techniques they discovered have led to curricular reform on many campuses as the powerful tool of writing has come to play a more central role in student learning in all fields. If you are at a campus that has developed a program in writing across the curriculum or has specially designated intensive writing courses, then you are participating in this revision of collegiate education. Even if you aren't, you can use the techniques yourself to improve your learning.

The techniques remain good ways to learn to write, as well. Because they give immediate help in reaching the goals of your other classes, they also give your writing a clear, directly visible purpose—to help you learn. Writing for your own private benefit often seems easier, and what you learn about writing, as well as what you learn about the subject, lasts better.

In addition, if you learn something while you are writing, your writing cannot help but be improved. You know something at the end that you didn't know at the beginning (perhaps because the writing has made you pay attention in a new way, as even paraphrasing can do), and you can offer that same experience of growth to your reader. You know where you were before writing, and you know what changed as you learned. So using writing as a tool for learning helps you learn to write in this way too.

Finally, using writing to learn can build your confidence. When you are playing this particular game, or using this particular tool, you do not necessarily know what the consequences will be. Writing can surprise you. If you allow it to do that when you write to learn in your classes, you will be more likely to trust your writing when you employ it elsewhere.

ACTIVITY 5–2: USING WRITING TO LEARN

Three activities that many people have found especially helpful with their learning are described below. You should try them until you find the one through which you actually learn something.

Freewriting

Freewriting is described in Activity 4–4 in Chapter Four. You do it exactly the same way here: write as fast as you can for a set period of time, eight or ten minutes. Do not pause, but keep writing rapidly. Don't even think about punctuating, organizing, correcting, making it legible, or anything else that might get in the way of the free flow.

The variable is *when* you use it. If you get a chance, use it in the middle of a class in another subject. If you just write for five minutes as fast as you can about what you are hearing, what you think about it, what you think it might mean, you can get a whole new orientation on the subject. Two other especially productive times to use freewriting, if you don't want to interrupt the class, are immediately before the class, when you try to predict what will happen, and immediately after, when you summarize, extend, apply, or perhaps argue with what you have just heard.

This type of learning seems to work because freewriting is quick and uncensored; it allows you to bring into your awareness things that you might have noticed without knowing you did so, or find connections you didn't know you had made, or spot problems you might otherwise have failed to recognize. Writing makes these things present and visible, and thereby useful to you.

Journals

Journals can be used simply as storage for freewriting, and they have powerful effects when used this way. They have some other effects, too, because they allow for reflection and analysis.

Journals can be tailored to suit you, and they should be, because the benefits come from activities that make sense to you. The suggestions in the following list are ways in which people have taken advantage of journalkeeping just in an academic context (journals have powerful effects in personal contexts, as well):

1. If you have two classes on related themes, write in the journal about the connections and overlaps you notice. Or if one class last term led to one you are now taking, you could refer to the old notes to see how they connect to the new material. Or perhaps you can write about a contrast between the way a subject was handled in high school and how it is presented in your college class.

2. As you take notes on some reading for a class, use only the left-hand pages for the actual notes. Use the right-hand side for comments, anticipations, noticing repetitions, finding connections to other parts of the reading or the course, questions, and especially disagreements.

3. If you know what the topic of a future lecture is, prepare a minilecture on the topic yourself from sources not presented in the class. Then you can merely keep track of where the actual lecture material differs from your predictions. (This technique is sometimes called overlearning, and it is particularly useful in introductory courses, such as introductions to psychology, sociology, art history, and so on, where differences in approach can make a big difference in the content of the course.)

Once you have had a successful learning experience through a journal activity, you have some new information about how writing can help you learn. Is it that writing can give you both the time to reflect and also the impulse to formulate in words the results of reflection?

Microthemes

Using material from any course, compose a list of 10–12 propositions that bear on but do not decide an important issue in the course. If you are studying natural resources, for example, you might encounter the issue of whether there really is an energy shortage. Propositions that bear on this issue but do not decide it might include these:

1. 90% of the world's oil is still in the ground—2.1 trillion barrels.
2. The proportion of oil left in the U.S. is much less than 90%.
3. Experts estimate that the U.S. will ultimately produce a total of 204 billion barrels of oil.
4. The U.S. has produced and burned 110 billion barrels of oil so far.
5. Et cetera.
6. Et cetera.
7. Et cetera.
8. Et cetera.
9. We have used 1.7% of the world's coal supply.
10. Coal smoke is a serious air pollutant.

11. Coal burning leaves much ash.
12. Et cetera.

Once you have isolated the factual propositions and stated them in neutral terms (you might want to check these with someone else in the class to see whether they really are neutral), you are ready to write the microtheme. You might decide that there really *is* an energy shortage because the objections to coal seem decisive and because you interpret the rate of oil discovery and consumption as accelerating. You might decide there is *not* an energy crisis because the problems with coal will be solved when it becomes economically useful to solve them. Or perhaps you take some modified position, such as that it is only the United States that has an energy crisis. Whatever you decide basically involves attaching significance to the different facts and deciding how they fit together to determine an answer to the issue.

Completing a microtheme exercise has some unique benefits. For one thing, we are accustomed to taking facts as already significant in themselves, and so they are sometimes. But nearly all facts can be stated in a variety of ways, and it can give a paper a tremendous argumentative advantage if you show that you can state the facts in fair and unbiased ways before you go on to illustrate your interpretation. Readers naturally resist facts that seem to be stated in slanted ways even if they accept the position the writer is arguing for, so the effort spent on stating facts fairly can be well spent.

Another benefit of this activity is that it helps focus our attention on the facts that really support positions. In constructing a microtheme about the energy crisis from the preceding list of propositions, the people who think there is a crisis nearly always put some special emphasis on statements about the accelerating use of oil and the problems with coal, while those who think there isn't a crisis tend to stress the amount of energy reserves that remain.

THE IMPORTANCE OF OTHER PEOPLE

We have already noticed ways in which other people can help improve our writing by helping generate ideas. Many writers report that they might play a more central role, as well.

ACTIVITY 5–3: AN INTERVIEW

One advantage of learning in a classroom, which you might already have experienced in the anthology assignments in earlier chapters, is that a group of people can gather much more information, and generally better information, much faster than one person can gather it. In this activity, you will be gathering information in a research group on how people have learned to write.

Procedure

Your contribution will be to interview someone who writes. This person need not be a professional writer, say a journalist or newspaper reporter or a technical writer, but it should be someone who writes for more than personal reasons (e.g., in personal letters, a journal or diary, schedules and lists, and so on). You might select someone working in a career you would enjoy or in one you want to explore. You might select a friend of a friend: an accountant, engineer, public information officer, police officer, researcher, advertising writer, lawyer, lab technician, nurse, or a teacher from another of your classes. I have learned from experience that you should *not* use friends or relatives and should do your best to avoid people you already know; for one thing, you will learn less about interviewing, and for another, if you are already familiar with that person, your established lines of communication might either prevent you from asking relevant questions or shape and even distort the answers you get.

The interview should focus on how the person you choose learned to write what the job requires, although you will also need to find out what exactly the writing amounts to—samples would be very helpful. My suggestion for a central question turns up in a surprising number of interviews: Was there a single person who taught the person you are interviewing to write by paying special attention to his or her writing over some period of time? (If there was such a person, you might also want to ask about the writer's attitude toward this help.)

Preliminary Discussion

With these goals in mind, your class or writing group can work out detailed instructions about the right ways of making contact with suitable interviewees, of asking for the interview, of planning the questions to ask and the order in which to ask them, of thanking the interviewee for his or her time, and of presenting the results orally or in writing. For example, asking open questions like "What kind of writing do you do?" is generally more productive than asking yes/no questions like "Did you learn to write in school?" Another decision your group or class should make is whether the people interviewed are enough alike for a single report or two to express what almost everyone finds out, or whether there is going to be great diversity, in which case it might be most useful to all the members of the class to hear about or read each interview report.

Writing

Write up your interview in a shortened form that eliminates unnecessary material and quotes the most useful material directly from the person interviewed.

Discussion

Read your interview report to your group or class. What generalizations seem to stand up through all this information?

CRITICAL THINKING

People who set out to improve their writing must be prepared to admit that they need to change their habits, add new strategies, expand their repertoire, stop doing some of the things they have always done, and so on. This is not an easy attitude to develop. We tend to see our writing as a reflection of ourselves—as it is to some extent—and to think that imperfections in our writing must mean imperfections in ourselves, which can be painful to admit. Taking a critical attitude toward our writing is closely related to what we might call critical thinking, the practice of examining any piece of writing for its doubtful assumptions, excessive generalizations, questionable connections and support of points, unwarranted assertions of significance, and so on.

It is not easy to exercise critical thinking on ourselves. But if some kind of critical thinking is so useful to so many people learning to write, it is surely worth trying. Here is how one person went about it:

About this time I met with an odd volume of the *Spectator* [a magazine of the time, like today's *The New Yorker* in some ways and like *People* magazine in others]. It was the third. I had never before seen any of them. I bought it, read it over and over, and was much delighted with it. I thought the writing excellent, and wished, if possible, to imitate it. With this view I took some of the papers, and making short hints of the sentiments in each sentence, laid them by a few days, and then, without looking at the book, try'd to compleat [*sic*] the papers again, by expressing each hinted sentiment at length, and as fully as it had been expressed before, in any suitable words that should come to hand. Then I compared my *Spectator* with the original, discovered some of my faults, and corrected them.

The writer is Benjamin Franklin, discussing one of the ways in which he improved his writing in a passage from more than 250 years ago. It is not quite accurate to say that he was teaching himself to write, because he was modeling his writing on that of the *Spectator,* which he so admired, learning to think the way its writers did and to express himself as they did. He designed his own exercises and corrected them himself, which is important (see the next section of this chapter). But he began with admiration, with the belief that someone else could write better than he could, and that he could stand improvement.

In the most profound sense, writers improve when they begin to admit that they might be wrong, that what seems to be so might not be so, that the truth might be out of reach for now and approximations all that can be put down. Writing must be provisional, which means that it is the best one can do for now, always allowing for the possibility that it can be improved in ideas and expression later. Critical thinking helps to improve one's writing particularly if one is able to articulate these kinds of doubts clearly along with one's own points. Such critical thinking sometimes takes the form of deciding how certain you are of what you are saying. You make a recommendation about what your department at work should be doing, and you say somewhere in it that you are mostly convinced, or pretty sure, or only speculating—these are ways of indicating how you think your ideas will stand up to the critical standards you think other people will apply to your suggestion. But there are other ways of managing the critical dimension of writing too, like Franklin's way of simply writing against a standard of excellence you desire to attain.

ACTIVITY 5–4: ARGUING WITH YOURSELF

Take a short selection of your writing from your journal, from freewriting, or from a finished essay. It can even be a short paragraph if it develops an idea through several sentences. The important thing is that it set forth a point of view. Write a point-by-point draft that disputes as many of the points in the original selection as possible and that argues particularly against the examples or other support for the main point. Notice particularly whether stating these arguments helps you have some sympathy for them. Can you write a revised passage that includes both sides of this argument with yourself? Can you see how such a revision could be stronger than either of the originals?

There is a curious symmetry here among three of the major concerns of this book—reading, revising a particular composition, and improving one's writing skills. In reading critically, a reader makes meaning by anticipating, filling gaps, checking expectations, supplying examples, wondering about what's been left out, objecting, and so on. Similarly, in revising, a writer asks what readers will be anticipating, what gaps are being left, what misleading hints might have been given, what other examples might be supplied, how one point connects to other points, whether the stated points are oversimplified or even wrong. And just as readers and individual pieces of writing improve, so too does a writer. Writers improve by incorporating their doubts—based on experience with other people—into a good revision and by making these doubts into habits of mind. They must ask: How good is my evidence? How helpful are my illustrations? How convincing are the connections I make between my experience and my conclusions? These are empty questions until they carry full critical weight, and then they become the means by which writers improve as Franklin did.

A FINAL NOTE: TEACHING YOURSELF TO WRITE

The quick answer to how people learn to write is that they teach themselves. People who make up their own drills get the most out of them, because like all of us, they remember what they do so much better than what they see or hear. Similarly, people who deliberately imitate, like Franklin, get the most out of models. And, finally, people who admit they need improvement develop the best critical thinking.

The process of teaching oneself to write never comes to an end. Franklin was already something of a writer when he began working with the *Spectator*, and he could have simply continued as he was. But he knew what many writers come to know, that writing for different situations and audiences—and for different purposes— often in effect requires writers to learn to write all over again. It is apparently the attitude of writers who expect to keep learning that separates the truly effective from the barely competent.

PART THREE

RETHINKING WRITING

In Chapters Six through Nine, you will work on persuasion, reasoning, structure, and words and sentences. Each topic is meant to help you focus more sharply on the aspects of your writing that you can develop with greatest effect.

As you read, you can revise one of the drafts you wrote for Parts One or Two, or you can work with a completely new piece of writing that you will take through several drafts as you complete the activities in these chapters.

CHAPTER 6

How Writing Persuades

THE POINT OF THIS CHAPTER

When we think of *persuasion,* we probably think of it from the persuader's point of view. We might think of changing someone's mind by arguments, examples, reasons, or authority. We might think of imposing our view on someone else or at least trying to use all available means for doing so. We might even suppose that there are magic keys to persuasion that will enable us to have our way with audiences.

If we think of persuasion from the receiver's point of view, we probably think of advertisements, which seem to play on hidden motives to get us to buy things we otherwise wouldn't. We might think of juries under the spell of clever lawyers who somehow get them to ignore facts and laws in favor of their clients.

Seen in those ways, persuasion is an all-or-nothing affair. As a persuader, you either win or lose; as a receiver, you are either susceptible or immune to the persuasive effort. And learning to persuade means learning some tricks, some devices to insert into one's argument.

This book presents a different view of persuasion. We have said that writing is half a conversation or the script for a conversation with enough guidance for the reader to tell that things are going according to plan. When we speak in a conversation, we claim the hearer's interest, and we imply that what we are saying is interesting, relevant, maybe useful or entertaining, worth hearing about. If we succeed in getting people to hear us out, then we have persuaded them that what we said had these qualities.

Similarly, when we write for an audience, we attempt to get the reader to keep reading, to participate in the conversation, and then if possible to accept what we are saying. We claim that what we are saying is important, relevant, believable and useful in some way, or at least interesting. And if we convince our readers that our writing contains all these qualities, then we have successfully used persuasion.

So persuasion isn't a bag of tricks that we can acquire after we have learned many other things about writing. As soon as we start writing for an audience, we are essentially engaged in various kinds of persuasive efforts. This idea can be very intimidating if we take it to mean that we must change people's minds completely every time we write.

But of course we do not have to change people's minds completely every time we write, any more than we do every time we speak. In a conversation, people's ideas may change only a very small bit, or very slowly. Similarly, in writing, we can be satisfied simply to raise a doubt, make a suggestion, show another point of view, or achieve some other equally modest goal. We don't have to change readers' opinions 180 degrees; 5 degrees would be a substantial change. We don't need techniques for all-out assaults, either; instead, we need ways of finding common ground, points of agreement, and a vocabulary acceptable to everyone.

In this chapter, we look at writing as essentially persuasive, and we see how persuasion actually operates from the reader's point of view. In the next chapter, we look at persuasion from the writer's point of view to see how people use *reasoning* in the writing process. For now, we deal with a broader question: How do writers get readers to keep on reading?

ON BEING PERSUADED

Cases of total persuasion do exist, of course, cases in which someone's mind is changed 180 degrees. There is in English literature a famous example of an extreme case of total persuasion. It occurs in Jane Austen's *Pride and Prejudice* when the heroine, Elizabeth, reads a letter written to her by Mr. Darcy in which he overturns her prejudices against him and in favor of Mr. Wickham.

> When she read with somewhat clearer attention, a relation of events, which, if true, must overthrow every cherished opinion of [Mr. Wickham's] worth . . . her feelings were yet more acutely painful and more difficult of definition.
>
> Astonishment, apprehension, and even horror, oppressed her.*

Elizabeth is confused and upset because Darcy has written that Wickham is a scoundrel and that she herself has been both proud and prejudiced—prejudiced in favor of Wickham, prejudiced against Darcy, too proud to think that things might be other than as they seem to her. That is not the kind of letter one would expect her to continue reading, because it gives so unpleasant a picture of herself, but she does read on, for reasons we are to infer.

> She wished to discredit it [the letter from Mr. Darcy] entirely, repeatedly exclaiming, "This must be false! This cannot be! This must be the grossest falsehood!"—and when she had gone through the whole letter, though scarcely knowing anything of the last page or two, put it hastily away, protesting that she would not regard it, that she would never look in it again. . . .

Elizabeth resists the letter, denies it, tries to hold to her previous opinions—but she does read to the end. Somehow she has already begun to admit that she might have been wrong, and it is this virtue that Austen wished to claim above all others for her heroine.

> . . . but it would not do; in half a minute the letter was unfolded again, and collecting herself as well as she could, she again began the mortifying perusal of all that related to Wickham, and commanded herself so far as to examine the meaning of every sentence. . . .

Elizabeth submits to this mortification because she can conceive of being wrong, of needing to be persuaded, but it is very unpleasant. So far it has been oppressive, "acutely painful,"

*All quotations from *Pride and Prejudice* are from pages 153–157 of the Mark Schorer edition. Boston: Houghton Mifflin, 1956.

horrifying to consider that she has been completely wrong. But she "collects" herself and "commands" herself, and these words say how difficult it is for her to keep reading at the same time that they express Austen's view that there has to be something in the reader that is stronger than those difficult feelings, some engagement of the self, or some values to which the heroine will hold even if holding to them is acutely painful. To collect yourself and command yourself means holding to these values, which are, in Elizabeth's case, a desire to know the truth, to judge people accurately, and to see herself as other see her.

> How differently did everything now appear. . . . She grew absolutely ashamed of herself.—Of neither Darcy nor Wickham could she think without feeling that she had been blind, partial, prejudiced, absurd. . . . [She wandered] along the lane for two hours, giving way to every variety of thought; re-considering events, determining probabilities, and reconciling herself as well as she could to a change so sudden and so important. . . .

Such a painful experience is what we all fear when we think about persuasion. Almost against her will, Elizabeth is brought to see the truth of things, and even though it is the truth she comes to, and even though she knows she is now doing the right thing, she is deeply ashamed because earlier she had been so badly in error. Total persuasion makes of her a different woman in some respects; she knows she will have to behave differently in the future, and will not only have to make apologies and amends, but will also have to guard against making her old mistakes again.

Persuasion like this must be extremely rare. But even in this case we can see that persuasion depends on something in the reader—Elizabeth's willingness to consider Darcy's words. In every case of persuasion, something can be learned about the means by which people can be brought to see something they did not see before. Seeing things from the receiver's point of view generally provides the key.

ACTIVITY 6-1: MEANS OF PERSUASION

The point of this activity is to examine from the receiver's point of view what it is like to be persuaded (in a much less drastic fashion than in Jane Austen's example). If you can identify the means of persuasion in an example taken from your own experience and add your view to those of others, you can come to a better understanding of how persuasion actually works.

Procedure

The first step is to get the right kind of experience. Not everyone can do this easily; some people respond to the question of "How were you persuaded?" by saying that they have *never* been persuaded of anything in their lives. But most of us can remember a time when someone changed our minds about something. Sometimes we might realize we have been persuaded, for instance, without knowing at the time even that we had been, let alone knowing how, we were persuaded.

To describe the experience in a useful way, I think you need to do these things:

1. Write about the experience as a "before-and-after" situation, as in the diet ads.
2. As you write, try very hard to make the "before" believable. (Since it is the idea you have given up, this may take effort).
3. Examine as if under a microscope exactly how the change was made. The more detail you can put down here, the more useful your contribution to the group's understanding will be. Did someone show you that you were making an error? How? Was the new view more in your interest than the old? Was there an appeal to some ideal that you held? How did the "after" ideas seem to fit better with yourself than the "before" ones, even if changing was to some extent difficult?

Quite often we are barely aware that persuasion has occurred. That "barely" might be the most important aspect of the phenomenon of persuasion. It means two things: first, our minds aren't generally changed in sweeping ways so much as they are slightly modified. Perhaps we come to believe something a bit more strongly than we used to, or perhaps we believe something a bit less surely. Perhaps we see that our former view was roughly accurate but just too simple to fit the facts of the case. Second, the means by which we were moved are often just extensions of the ways we normally think anyway.

Slight modifications and extensions of how we usually think: if these are the essence of persuasion, then we can see what Jane Austen saw, that from the receiver's point of view, persuasion is really self-persuasion. Someone else gives us the means, but we ourselves supply the necessary momentum. From the writer's point of view, then, persuasion doesn't mean overpowering the reader but rather providing means for someone to use in changing his or her mind. What Darcy did was appeal to Elizabeth's "better instincts," her need to know the truth and her wish to be fair, to get her to listen to his side of the events.

This appeal to better instincts obviously has to start from common ground, from an assumed (and actual) agreement between the writer and the reader that values like the truth and fairness are important. These values rarely need to be stated, but it is often important for writers to keep in mind the common ground to which they are appealing.

CLASSICAL RHETORIC

As your class examines the cases of persuasion they have collected, they might well find means of persuasion few other people have noticed. Some of the more familiar means I have heard people list are these:

Someone showed me that I was being inconsistent.

Someone showed me I already acted as though I believed what he was saying.

She just showed me how other people have thought about my problem.

I heard how [someone famous] did this.

The other person conceded a point, so I did too.

The person who sold it to me was very nice and quite helpful.

I couldn't have bought it if I had waited.

I realized I wasn't a child any more, and I needed to start acting like who I really was.

There are many such patterns of change, and they are worth examining because they help writers see just how readers actually change their minds.

The field of *rhetoric* undoubtedly got its start when some observant person noticed an effective pattern of persuasion and developed some advice from the observation. In fact, a common definition of rhetoric, based on Aristotle's, is "the art of finding the available means of persuasion in any situation."

We could give several pieces of rhetorical advice just on the basis of the preceding list. We could suggest creating an attractive "voice" and implied speaker so that, as writers, we sound like people worth listening to. We could also recommend writing as though we respected our readers so they can participate in the conversation without feeling insulted. We could recommend working from ideas already held by the audience, by natural extension of the ways they already think. As is always the case with advice, of course, the problem is not so much getting it as taking it, making it work in a particular situation.

In Greece more than two millennia ago, the forms of government that evolved for small city-states required considerable public speaking and public debate. Three situations in particular seemed to generate most of the argument: deciding what future policy should be, deciding what present value a certain event or person had, and deciding whether some past act or event had been right or wrong. In each of the situations, philosophers noticed that one could find much the same elements of persuasion as in the others. Effective speakers relied on a few basic means for getting their points across. These basic means and their explanation make up what is now called *classical rhetoric*. It includes the work of Greeks like Plato and Aristotle and of Romans like Cicero and Quintilian.

The fact that their few basic points are still around today suggests that early rhetoricians must have found out something about human nature rather than just about their particular cultures. You can discover the basic points for yourself. One way is to read with close attention and compare your experience with that of others; as your ideas grow and change, you will be demonstrating the "means of persuasion" the rhetoricians talk about.

Another way to discover some of these basic means of persuasion is to look at an actual example of a decision you have made. The hypothesis of the next activity is that you chose the school you now go to for some persuasive reasons. You almost certainly discussed these reasons with people before you came, and in fact you probably developed a kind of shorthand way of explaining the reasons. This shorthand would have been particularly useful in situations in which you didn't have much time to explain yourself but had to give someone a quick idea of how you made the choice you did.

ACTIVITY 6-2: RHETORICAL ANALYSIS

The shorthand you used to discuss your decision to come to your present school would have been especially useful at parties, perhaps with the people you went to high school with or socialized with before coming to your present school. You almost certainly had to develop some kind of "party talk," some quick and easy, possibly amusing way of telling other people where you were going and why.

Procedure

First, write out a sample (a real one if you can remember, or an approximate one if you can't) of this party talk in which you and perhaps some other people explain why they are going to particular schools.

Next, find in the catalog of your college, usually in the first thirty to fifty pages, the general statements designed to explain to all kinds of readers why people attend this school and what its particular strengths are. These statements might refer to its location, its setting, its physical plant, its physical relation to a community, its origins, the reasons for its founding, its illustrious graduates, its reputation, its strong departments or areas of study, its unique atmosphere, its special programs, its costs or support of students through scholarships or other aid, and so on. Collect as much of this material as you can; photocopying might be the easiest way to assemble it.

Using your party talk as an entry point, figure out whether the writers of the college catalog were aware of your reasons for choosing the school. Were they able to appeal to potential students using your kind of reason? What other reasons do they give that influenced your decision even though they didn't fit into your party talk? Are the writers of the catalog able to say things that *could not* be expressed in party talk? Or do you find things in the party talk that could never appear in the catalog?

Writing

Analyze the two kinds of reasons—your own and the one that appears in the catalog—for attending a school. What value is being appealed to? Is it the value of obtaining a good bargain, a good service for the money? Is it prestige? Is it the authority of important people who say that the school is a good one? Is it convenience?

Once you have identified the type of appeal, you can usually see clearly the *value* it appeals to. Costs that will fit within the budget of prospective attendees appeal to thrift; reputation that will give graduates a boost in their careers appeals to ambition, and special programs that will lead to special competence appeal to a different value.

Even in a more detailed rhetorical analysis than this activity called for, the basic elements remain the same. Taking a piece of writing apart rhetorically means examining the means of persuasion the writer employs. These means usually involve how writers present themselves, how they characterize their audience, or how they arrange their material.

From a reader's point of view, analyzing the rhetoric of a college catalog means looking at the way the writers of the catalog try to find common ground with readers. The writers of the catalog have a tremendously difficult job, of course, because a wide variety of readers will be using the catalog—high school guidance counselors and teachers, prospective students, the parents of prospective students, alumni, admissions officers at the school and at other schools, college faculty and administrators—for a wide variety of purposes—deciding whether to refer or recommend students, deciding whether to attend, deciding whether to support or oppose the choice of the school for someone else, selecting students who will profit from attending, shaping course goals and programs.

Because it addresses such a wide audience with so many reasons for reading it, the college catalog must of necessity seem somewhat distanced from the individual concerns of most readers. Much material will be irrelevant or will appeal to values held by someone else. Sometimes these effects can be seen in people's party talk as well, of course.

HOW PEOPLE CHANGE THEIR MINDS

Have you ever wondered what makes other people so stubborn? Let us suppose you have been arguing with someone, trying to convince him or her of the truth as you see it. You try everything. You show the other person in great detail all the reasons why you believe the point, you show why the other person should believe it, you give good grounds for believing it, you show it's in the other person's interest to believe it, you show that the other person already acts as if he or she believed it, you mention some other people who believe it—and you get nowhere. It's easy to conclude that the other person in this case must be irrational, nuts, so stubborn that he or she "won't listen to reason."

Psychologists have wondered about this phenomenon also, and have studied the occasions on which people actually do change their minds. People *can* change their minds because of arguments, or course; many of us can remember being talked into or out of things. But far more frequent than reasoning into or out of a conclusion on an examination of grounds or interests, apparently, is change of mind based on how the new belief fits with previously held beliefs, what psychologists call *coherence*. We change our minds most easily when we can see how the new belief fits with other things we already believe.

To the person being persuaded, this sort of persuasion doesn't appear to be very manipulative. It seems a natural extension of certain things within us, even if those things are at odds with other things as they were for Jane Austen's Elizabeth. Despite the mortification of admitting she was wrong, Elizabeth is able to use the values she really holds most dear—her love of truth and her desire to evaluate herself and all other people accurately—to interpret the events in which she has been participating, however blindly.

In general, people are rarely overwhelmed or led into conclusions they could never have come to themselves. We seem to have a built-in principle of economy, which allows us to make only the smallest possible adjustment in our beliefs and plans to accommodate any new idea; if it requires great changes, we generally won't accept it without a long struggle requiring strong motivation.

Why are we this way? The causes are not mysterious. We cannot get very far in life if we continually change our minds to a large extent. We cannot always be remembering the grounds on which we decided to accept some point a year ago, another point five years ago, and another related point last week. Our brains, however vast, are still finite, our time is limited, and we have to avoid mental clutter if we possibly can. So we don't generally evaluate all our beliefs when a new belief is suggested to us; instead, we look for the smallest possible adjustment that will square things. Sometimes this means rejecting the new item—and there we are, being stubborn ourselves. Stubbornness, resistance to persuasion when *we* are the ones being stubborn in fact feels like being reasonable, like being efficient, like reviewing our situation as thoroughly as we can given the limitations of time, memory, and effort we always face.

If that is why we are stubborn, it is probably also why other people are stubborn. When we are writing, we need to assume that our audience will be stubborn in exactly the same way we would be. Our readers will resist accepting the changes that we suggest unless we can show how our views fit with views the readers already accept. For readers to do otherwise would be uneconomical. If we think of writing as changing views, then, we are less likely to make excessive claims, less likely to restate the obvious, and more likely to extend our own writing until it makes a genuine contribution to the reader's views.

BEING PERSUADED AND REVISING

There is a close connection between being persuaded and revising one's own writing. Both involve slight changes and adjustments, and both are subject to strong limitations. But there is a closer relation as well. We revise our positions, beliefs, and statements when we are persuaded, and we revise them when we rework our own writing also.

Consider how you become convinced that something you have written needs changing. You read it over a few days after writing, and you say to yourself, "That doesn't say quite what I meant." Perhaps you formulate an alternative sentence or two, then realize a word from your first version fits the second version and really does say better what you intended, provided you leave out some of the rest of the first version. This sort of thing happens continually to all writers as they revise. How is it possible to change your mind this way?

It's as if you begin by admitting that you could be wrong. In writing, you get a chance to review more than you ordinarily can, to entertain ideas and hypotheses you might not otherwise consider, to explore the relationship between new and old ideas in more detail than you otherwise could. In all these ways, you admit that limitations or mistakes are possible, just as you do when you change your mind. And so, in effect, you persuade yourself into being smarter than you were, into knowing more or knowing something better because you have been willing to be wrong.

Most importantly, writing that has been revised has the best chance of persuading other people. That fact has occurred to many writers, who say things like "easy writing makes hard reading," or "writing is 95 percent revision." What they mean is that the work of making writing effective is just getting started when you have identified your interest, discovered your connection with a topic, and generated your new ideas about it.

The work that follows, which is called "re-vision" because it usually means literally re-seeing your thoughts, is best character-ized as persuading yourself to see how your idea corresponds to the knowledge and beliefs of other people. To accomodate this revised view of your idea, you usually discover the means by which other people can "revise" their way toward it also. In other words, you can imagine persuading your readers to revise their ideas just as you revised yours.

CONNECTING AND SEPARATING IDEAS

One of the main ways we change our minds is by continually looking at how ideas fit together. We begin by thinking that we have said it all. But the "it," however complete it may be in itself, cannot be presented in a vacuum. We see ideas that attach, that are implied or contained, that follow in some way from the one we started with. Connecting ideas in this way or separating ideas usually seen as connected is also one of the main ways people revise their writing.

For example, using the microtheme technique from Activity 5–2, a writer identifies neutral propositions about teenage parents. Here are some of them:

1. More than a quarter of a million infants are born to unmarried teenagers every year. . . .

3. Nearly 10,000 of the mother are 14 or younger.

4. Two-thirds of teenaged mothers are white.

7. Approximately 97 percent of today's unmarried teen mothers who deliver choose to keep their babies.

10. To some girls, the idea of having a baby gives their life meaning—someone to love and be loved by in return.

11. Teenagers get pregnant and give birth for a variety of reasons, but most have unrealistic ideas of what it's like to raise a baby.

And so on. I have selected the propositions that supported the writer's view of teenage parents, which she expressed in the familiar phrase "Children Who Have Children." As she assembled her microtheme (and the research paper that later evolved out of it), she established a *link,* a connection between two ideas, that gave her view extra power. The link was between the ages of the parents and the babies; she chose her phrase to put together two ideas in the same word "children." This was one of the ways she sought to persuade her readers that the situation of teenage mothers is difficult and that something should be done. Her method of persuasion was to connect ideas, the one she assumed her readers already accepted (that the new infants are children) with the one they might not have thought of (that the parents are really children themselves). Her connection is powerful because we generally do not think that children are capable of raising other children.

Persuasion can work in the reverse direction as well. People working in AIDS education have put much effort into separating the idea of AIDS from that of homosexual activity, a link that was unfortunately established some years ago and now seems to the writers to be contributing to the spread of the disease. People will take adequate precautions, they argue, only if they see that the threat of AIDS is more general.

If you want to see your writing as someone else will see it, you must consider the connections and disconnections between ideas. Even if your topic is a personal essay, you will want to look at what is going to be familiar to your readers and what is going to establish a new connection. One of the most famous of all personal essays, E. B. White's "Once More to the Lake," works from a vacation trip to a lake with the writer's son to a memory of trips with his father, and eventually makes a connection between being a son and being a father. The significance in the writer's experiences lies precisely in the connections, overlaps, the near-identity, established between the two ideas usually kept distinct.

The connections and disconnections of ideas represent the

conceptual side of what you try to accomplish when you write for readers. You cannot expect to change people's minds totally, but you can expect to move them a little bit if you work from points or ideas you expect your readers to accept to new ones you want them to accept.

CONCLUDING ACTIVITY: REVISING AND PERSUADING

From your journal or freewriting, or elsewhere if you prefer, find something you have written that you would like to revise. The piece should be on a personal subject that could be made significant for others. Look particularly for the chance to connect familiar experience with new experience, an old idea with a new one.

After revising your work in this way, read the paper to a small group. Ask the group to identify the ideas you are connecting or separating.

CHAPTER 7

How People Reason

THE POINT OF THIS CHAPTER

When we think of *reasoning* sometimes we think of *formal logic*. We distinguish "deduction" from "induction." We worry about "fallacies." We use words like "rigorous," "prove," "therefore," and "valid." To show the connections between one sentence and another, we may represent the sentences with letters and use other characters for the relations between them, an algebraic approach that leads to *symbolic logic*.

When we are actually reasoning, however, as opposed to analyzing reasoning that has already been done, something quite different goes on. Formal logic may supply us with tools for examining arguments, but it is not intended to teach us the processes by which arguments are discovered. Nor are the kinds of argument we actually use in conversation and writing limited to the few that can be formalized and shown always to compel readers' assent. In fact, we very seldom have such arguments available.

One philosopher has looked at reasoning in this way: if certainty or validity were *possible* in our daily arguments, we probably wouldn't have many arguments in the first place. We argue, we reason, and we try to show others our reasoning in situations where things are not self-evident, where we cannot prove our points in a rigorously valid deduction. All the apparatus of formal logic has its use, but no one has yet figured out how to use it to get to good arguments in the first place.

The view of reasoning presented in this chapter is meant to help you become aware of the ways in which you work your way toward good reasons. It is unlikely that you are unfamiliar with these strategies. You may not have realized how they apply to writing, however, so you are encouraged to try them out here.

WHAT IS AN ARGUMENT?

In common usage, an *argument* is a disagreement. People argue when communication between them has broken down. The argument is a struggle, like combat in some ways and perhaps even leading beyond words when tempers get too hot. Even if it remains verbal, this kind of argument isn't very productive. It often consists merely of opposing statements, like children's "did," "did not," "did so," "didn't."

At the other extreme, an argument in *formal logic* is a series of propositions in harmony with each other. The propositions are linked by special words so that if one accepts the premises (the statements that come first), one must accept the conclusion—or else contradict oneself. Argument in this sense is totally independent of participants and their views; it is so mechanical that computer programs can be written to check the connections.

Only certain elements of language allow this kind of precise, step-by-step procedure from "definitions" and "assumptions" to "conclusions" by means of "rules of inference." These elements include words like "and," "or," "not," "if," and "then." More advanced studies have worked out rules for "all" and "there is." Attempts to extend the formal procedures to "a" and "the," to "possibly" and "necessarily" have been made, but they are controversial. It turns out to require great analytic ability and tremendous patience to spell out exactly how these words can be used in arguments that lead to complete certainty. Through all these efforts, the words which are *not* carefully specified must be replaced with symbols that indicate they are being ignored.

Writers obviously cannot wait for logicians to complete their work on all words in the dictionary. We cannot expect to compel assent to our views, and we cannot ignore the participation of readers as we argue. Fortunately, we do not need to anticipate complete opposition, either.

We say of effective reasoning or argument when we read it that it is "telling," that a point is "well taken" or "cogent" or "insightful," that an example is "persuasive" or "suggestive." These words mean that we have moved as we read from some position to some new position. As Chapter Six showed, we may have no sense of combat. We may simply have seen some new complication we didn't see before, or a new connection we had missed between two facts; we may come to understand the benefit of thinking about some subject as if it were something else. From our point of view as readers, we often feel we have come to all these new positions voluntarily, rather than feeling compelled. Sometimes they feel like extensions or applications of thoughts we already have had.

Since as readers we don't expect (nor do we want) to be compelled, as writers we should not take compulsion as our standard either. Readers expect to hear the best arguments, presented in the best ways, but they will not ignore our writing just because it doesn't "prove" its point in the way that formal logic tries to guarantee. The writing of an effective argument means finding the best possible arguments for the reader, whom we as writers can assume to be reasonable, not unrealistic, in evaluating what we present. This chapter focuses on these reasonable arguments.

ACTIVITY 7–1: COLLECTING ARGUMENTS

If you live near a legislative or policymaking group of any kind, you can find actual arguments in great plenty. Attend a debate at a meeting of a local governmental committee, a student government, a city council meeting, or a school board. If you cannot find a live debate, perhaps a library near you is a governmental depository, and if so it should have the *Congressional Record*, in which you can find a debate on a topic that interests you. You can also find arguments of varying degrees of combativeness on some television shows (*The MacNeill/Lehrer Newshour*, William Buckley's *Firing Line*, and *Nightline*, for example).

Write down as much as you can of the argument as you understand it. Then draw some conclusions from what you observe. To what extent is it a genuine disagreement? Is there a resolution of any kind at the end? Do the participants seem to intend to reach agreement? Or do they "agree to disagree" in an amiable way? Or does this seem to be a pure disagreement?

The most interesting arguments for writers to observe are those in which the participants do not simply repeat the same points over and over, but instead look for ways to accommodate each other. When you see how people are willing to move from old positions to new ones, you get a sense of how a writer can sometimes help people to move from one belief to another, or from one point of view to another, for example.

PROBLEMSOLVING

Readers are much more likely to accept a writer's conclusions if they can see how the conclusions are arrived at. Writers who want their reasoning to appeal to readers take the time to make the steps of it clear. The next activity gives you a chance to focus on making steps clear.

ACTIVITY 7–2: SOLVING PROBLEMS OUT LOUD

Example

Consider the following question, which is like many of those given on SAT, ACT, Achievement, IQ, and other tests that purport to measure mental ability:

> Circle the letter after the letter in the word PENDULUM which is in the same position in the word as it is in the alphabet.

The first step is to read the problem carefully and agree on what it asks. It may have two or more parts, which must be written down (or remembered). In the case of this problem, there are two: find the letter in PENDULUM that is in the same position in the word as it is in the alphabet, and second, circle the letter in PENDULUM that is after that letter.

A working group might agree that the best way of completing the first step is to write the alphabet under the letters of pendulum, matching ABC to PEN. If you do that, you see that the fourth letter of PENDULUM is the fourth letter of the alphabet and that no other letter matches. So step one is complete.

The second is then to circle the letter after the D in PENDU-LUM, or U. Then the problem is complete.

The key, again, is to make each step explicit so that everyone can agree that it is correct. This is analogous to the writer's problem of showing a reader how to reach a particular conclusion.

Procedure

Here are four problems of different types for different groups in your class to solve in the same external, group-centered way. Each should report to the whole class on the agreed method of solution. If you have time, each group should make up more complicated problems of the same kind and present those to the class so that everyone can see firsthand how each type is best solved.

1. What should the next picture look like?

a) xxooxx
   ooxxoo

b) xoxoxox
   oxoxoxo

c) xxooxxoo
   ooxxooxx
   xxooxxoo
   ooxxooxx

d) ?

2. What is the next number in this series?

     5 11 19 29 41   ____

3. Wrist is to hand as ankle is to_____ .

4. Given two pitchers, one holding eight and one holding five gallons, and a hose to run water from, measure out one gallon.

Reflection

If you are like most people, you will feel a tremendous gain in certainty once you have worked these problems out with a group. There is something about a conclusion that several people agree on that inspires more confidence than one reached by one person in isolation. This increase in certainty has much to do with why people write—often, in addition to conveying information or a point of view or interpretation or recommendation, we want people to agree with us. We write, and if others understand and agree, even if only in part, we feel we are "on the right track" or "working along the right lines," or "headed in the right direction." This is a powerful effect of writing, one that many people find the most enduring reason to continue to improve their writing.

WHAT IS REASONING?

As writers, we must remember that we are not telling readers how to think. No one can tell anyone else in any definite way how he or she should think "any more than how he ought to breathe or to have his blood circulate," as John Dewey put it more than half a century ago. But the ways in which some writers think can be shown in their writing and described. Some of these ways are better than others, and, as Dewey added, "the reasons why they are better can be set forth."

Writers naturally want to understand why some ways of reasoning are better than others, and, to do this, they must learn to see better how other writers use reasoning to get from one sentence to another. In this section, I try to show the reasoning that underlies just a few sentences from a good writer. In fact, I'd say we value some writers and call them "good" partly because they show us how to reason about something.

A famous example is a writer who has had much influence on how we see our world—George Orwell. Here are the first two sentences of one of his famous essays, "Politics and the English Language":

> Most people who bother about the matter at all would admit that the English language is in a bad way, but it is generally assumed that we cannot by conscious action do anything about it. Our civilization is decadent and our language—so the argument runs—must inevitably share in the general collapse.

Another writer has said that the first word she writes limits the second, and the second the third, so that by the end of a couple of sentences, the entire essay is already determined. Something of this effect can be seen in Orwell's first two sentences because a great deal happens there. He asserts some things, takes others for granted, and indicates where he is trying to go in the essay—all in fifty-three words.

We might begin by taking a hint from "so the argument runs." In this phrase, Orwell makes it clear that he is presenting an argument with which he is going to disagree. The argument is that our language is in a bad way *because* our civilization is decaying and because (presumably), when a civilization decays, so does its language—inevitably. Orwell agrees that our language is in a bad way, but does not agree that it must be so.

That argument is spread through the first two sentences. In the first sentence, Orwell presents the position on which his opponents and the reader are assumed to agree, that the English language is in a bad way. We also get, in the "but " clause, the opponents' belief that nothing can be done about it, and Orwell's opinion about this belief, that it is "generally assumed." Since a general assumption is often questionable and is especially likely to be questioned if it appears in the opening sentence of an essay, the reader can be pretty sure that Orwell is going to attack the idea that nothing can be done about the sorry state of the English language. In this case, the position of the sentence helps us understand how Orwell wants us to take it.

What then does Orwell do in the second sentence? He explains that his opponents think the decline of English is the result of a decline of English civilization and asserts, with the word "inevitably," that the opponents think the connection between civilization and language is a necessary one.

It may seem that Orwell is going to a lot of trouble to set up his opponents' argument, using two sentences to establish their propositions and the connections between them. But Orwell knew very well what he was doing. He was a skilled journalist who made his living precisely through his interpretations of events and arguments, and he knew that if he did not raise these issues at the beginning of his essay, he would have little chance of making his readers as aware as he was of the problems he saw affecting the writing of English at that time. (He was writing shortly after the end of the Second World War, but the problems have not gone away, unfortunately.)

In his second sentence, he raises exactly the difficulty he faces in the essay, that his readers will find it more convenient, less trouble, simply to assume that nothing can be done to improve the way people express themselves in writing. He knew very well that this is not laziness on the part of his readers. He respected his readers and knew that his essay had to show why it would actually be more beneficial (in some way) to use extra effort in writing carefully. You cannot get someone to use extra effort unless you can show why it is in that person's interest to do so. And the real obstacle Orwell saw to his proposals for reforming the use of English was that it makes sense to people not to improve. Their approach to writing is already coherent: civilization is declining, and the language must decline too, so it doesn't matter if I express myself in a sloppy way. Orwell is trying to break a chain of beliefs that fit together very well already and substitute some others that will require more effort to live up to. That is a very difficult task, and Orwell is using all his resources to attempt it.

The relation between Orwell's two sentences is crucial, and it is a good example of the kind of reasoning that replaces formal patterns when we argue in words. What is the connection between the two sentences?

In the first, remember, Orwell lays out the position that everyone, himself included, agrees on: The English language is in a bad way. He also adds a contention that he doesn't accept: Nothing can be done. In the second sentence, he then describes two of his opponents' propositions that lead to this contention: (1) English civilization is in decay; (2) There is an inevitable connection between the decay of a civilization and the decay of a language. The second sentence explains the connection between the two propositions in the first: Because there is an inevitable connection between the decline of civilization and the decline of language, it is "inevitable" that the English language should decline as English civilization declines. It is this idea of inevitability that Orwell chooses to attack in explaining why he thinks something can indeed be done to improve the state of English.

Not many writers can manage so complicated an argument as Orwell can without confusing their readers. Orwell's journalistic training gave him that ability. It gave him the capacity to take on the most difficult issues and still expect to make some difference to his readers. It also gave him the ability to see into his opponents' positions as few writers have ever done, as the third sentence of his essay shows:

[1] Most people who bother about the matter at all would admit that the English language is in a bad way, but it is generally assumed that we cannot by conscious action do anything about it. [2] Our civilization is decadent and our language—so the argument runs—must inevitably share in the general collapse. [3] It follows that any struggle against the abuse of language is

a sentimental archaism [a foolish and emotional desire to return to archaic or old ways of life], like preferring candles to electric light or hansom cabs to airplanes.

Only the most skilled and confident writer can afford to give his opponents such powerful images as these: He lets his opponents say here that he—Orwell—prefers candles and horse-drawn cabs to electric lights and airplanes, that his desire to make the English language more effective is just as silly as such preferences would be.

Nor does he stop there. He finishes his first paragraph by saying, "Underneath this lies the half-conscious belief that language is a natural growth and not an instrument which we shape for our own purposes." He has pursued his opponents' position one step further, to focus on their belief about language which he can later demonstrate to be false. In a way, he had already demonstrated how *he* can shape language to his own purposes, since even while presenting his opponents' views, he has been able to give us a clear sense of what his own views are.

It is worth noting that Orwell does not have to state his own main idea or thesis in this first paragraph. Because of the relations among his sentences—adding in the second the idea of necessary connection in his opponents' view, in the third powerful images for their view, and in the fourth the belief that underlies the connection and the images—he has managed to get attentive readers to recognize his idea without saying it. This is doing two (or more) jobs at once, and doing them by eliciting the reader's reactions. These abilities are what have made Orwell a popular and influential writer even now, years after his death.

The lesson we can learn from Orwell is not that our arguments should be as complex as his. That complexity was his lifetime achievement, an attempt to do justice to complex thought. But we can learn how to watch for the connections between sentences as we read, and, as we write, we can be aware that these connections are under our control, "an instrument which we shape for our own purposes."

ACTIVITY 7–3: ANALYZING REASONING

From an argument on a subject with which you are familiar, choose your own passage to analyze. Examine the interconnections of the first four or five sentences, following the example given for Orwell. You should draw on all the background knowledge you need in order to make clear what the writer is arguing. What connections do you see between sentences?

___

It is as impossible to list all conceivable connections between sentences as it is to list all conceivable writers' personalities; we cannot take advantage of Orwell's ability just by imitating it (though that might get us started). Instead, we can develop our ability to connect sentences more and more effectively. The only general principle is that we must ultimately contribute to the coherence of our readers' beliefs by showing causes, effects, and other connections so that our arguments will have some chance of being accepted by readers just like us, who already have networks of beliefs and arguments in place in our heads.

THINKING ON PAPER

One similarity between our ordinary thinking and the thinking we do on paper is that both consist of successions of items. On paper, however, readers expect the connections of items to be more than accidental or "that reminds me." A writer presents an idea or example, readers assume, because it has consequences, because other things follow from it, are determined by it, and lead to other things. They expect some kind of consecutive order, each sentence in its right place, referring to its predecessors in some way and preparing for its followers. Readers do not expect to hear, "Now for something completely different."

In order to satisfy readers' demands for orderly reasoning and argumentation, we might have to make some adjustments in our ordinary thinking. One way to do so—very traditional advice in composition classes—is to "think through what you are going to say before you write it down." However, that is just what many of us *can't* do. Often we need to see some writing before we know what we really want to argue from and argue toward. The famous writer E. M. Forster said, "How do I know what I think until I see what I say?" So it is important to recognize, again, that people differ and that your preference as a writer probably lies somewhere between the extremes of people who know ahead of time what they want to argue and people who work it out as they go along.

If you are like the majority of writers, you might find yourself sometimes with a position you want to present and sometimes simply with some evidence in search of a position. Sometimes you know how your readers would like an idea developed, and sometimes you can only guess. Sometimes talking with a small group of sample readers—as in a class workshop—can help enormously at this point, for precisely the reasons you experienced as you solved problems in a group. You come to realize what people expect, what questions they are going to ask about your material that you hadn't foreseen, what hints you gave of directions in which you didn't go. You will get the most out of these conversations if you remember that you are learning how to do in your way what Orwell did in his—shape your language to help readers do what you want them to do.

PROBLEMFINDING

There are certain ways of looking at your own ideas that can contribute enormously to your effects on readers, to their perceptions of how reasonable you are and how compelling your writing is. Specifically, the answer to the question of how people reason is that they both solve problems (and enable others to solve them as we did) and *find* problems.

Orwell's opening paragraph, for example, certainly finds enormous problems: not only is the English language in bad shape, but also people have a strong argument about why nothing can be done. Within that framework he dramatizes his solutions to language problems, in the sense that they look dramatic because they overcome such obstacles. He creates the significance of his own ideas by stressing the opposition to them, which occupies most of the first paragraph of his essay. Without a clear expression of this significance, readers could have seen his essay as just some advice on how to write better without any serious claim on their attention.

ACTIVITY 7–4: PROBLEMFINDING AND REVISING

Background

You can work with any draft at this point. If you have gone through some of the generative activities you prefer, perhaps freewriting or journal writing or brainstorming or conversation or reading, and have found something you want to write about, and have written out for yourself in a draft what you want to say, then you are ready to revise in a problemfinding way.

Task

For this kind of revision, begin by stating the opposition to your draft as forcefully as possible.

Perhaps you chose the paper on indoor plants that came out of the fifty-specifics Activity 2–2. You begin by talking about plants being meant for the outdoors and the likelihood that readers who have tried to keep plants have lost some to neglect or overwatering or too much or too little sun—in short, with the difficulties.

Then you reframe your writing as a solution to these difficulties: You know a strategy that makes almost everyone successful at growing and enjoying house plants.

Notes

In this step you engage your readers by making clear to them why your writing matters. A writer can count on readers having certain interests and purposes—all of us want to increase our store of information, achieve our goals, or understand our world better. So we are interested in reading reports or accounts of things or places about which we have no experience, especially if these accounts come close to giving us the experience ourselves. We are interested in ways of getting things done better, so we read about how to do things we need to know how to do, and we read recommendations about making choices we need to make. We are also interested in insights into how our world works, including observations on what is more or less significant than we had thought.

This is a rather schematic account of readers' interests, but it shows what the real task of revision often is, especially if our writing has begun very personally, in private opinion and experience. Somehow we have to find ways to get readers to see what is valuable in our experience, and sometimes this means finding what is valuable in it for ourselves. Somehow we have to see our draft from the outside, take some new point of view on it, change our own view so that we can reasonably expect to change others' views by means of our writing.

USING EXAMPLES

One of the most common ways of making a point is to use an example. Inexperienced readers often object that an example doesn't prove the point it supports, and they are right. But examples are not supposed to *prove* a point, only to illustrate it and to show how the generalization applies to a specific instance.

Recently a student in one of my classes was writing an application to transfer to another college that had a program he had become interested in. The application asked him to write an essay about himself in which he was to tell the admissions office things that did not appear elsewhere on the application and would be useful in making the transfer decision. He thought immediately of his participation in track and decided that one of his examples would be the relays that were his specialty.

Simply listing the relays would probably have helped, since it was the kind of information required. But the student became worried because he realized that everyone seeking to transfer would probably have some activities to list. The admissions director wasn't just going to count activities and see who had the most; that would be unfair to those who participated in activities that take a lot of time. Would the director weight some activities more than others? But that would penalize some people because of their interests.

The student realized that the word "essay" might well be the important one in the question. The admissions director might very likely read applications to see what points people made in the process of listing the activities, even if those activities were simple ones like helping out at home or going beyond classroom assignments on occasion.

The examples that each applicant offered, then, would have to do several jobs at once. For one thing, they would indeed give the admissions director a chance to balance the class by admitting people with interests not already well represented. But they would also figure in a larger process. Could this prospective transfer student think clearly and significantly about the activities presented?

The student was in fact quite team-oriented. He had chosen the relays because he liked to work with others in reaching competitive excellence. He liked the training that required each runner to encourage the others, and he liked the thrill of doing his absolute best for a group rather than just for himself. He decided that he would try to bring out these preferences and interests through the discussion of his track experiences in order to show what kind of person and student he really was. (He was able to transfer, though this writing was clearly not the only reason.)

The examples he offered on the application were not only illustrations ("I am a well-rounded student; for instance, I run track."). They also presented a miniature piece of reasoning ("I am the kind of person who gets into an activity like track because I like individual effort within a team framework, etc."), and they suggested that the pattern of reasoning extended far beyond the particular activity into the kind of student he would make at the new school. The student was able to use some excellent detail from particular training sessions to show the qualities he wanted to present, and the examples backed him up 100 percent.

Examples, then, can contribute to a writer's argument. They can illustrate a point, which makes them valuable enough. But they can also have a larger effect, by showing how examples of their type fit the larger pattern: "I am the kind of student who . . ." These are the reasons examples are so powerful, even though they might not prove once and for all the point they support.

WHAT KINDS OF THINGS
DO PEOPLE REASON ABOUT?

We sometimes think that our job in an argument is to prove a point once and for all, beyond any shadow of a doubt. We want our arguments to meet a standard of absolute validity: It is impossible for the conclusion to be false if the preceding statements are true.

However, that standard is generally unattainable. It is unattainable because readers who disagree with a conclusion are always ready to question whether its supporting statements are true, and the less someone likes a writer's conclusions the more likely it is that he or she will challenge or reject those supporting statements. There are many ways around a conclusion one doesn't like.

The standard of guaranteed truth is also *inappropriate* to most of the arguments we write. If the truth could be guaranteed, it would either be obvious and self-evident or follow mechanically from points that themselves were self-evident or known to be true. But if it were self-evident or mechanically derivable, a point wouldn't need to be argued. We only argue and reason when we need to, when the answer isn't obvious or when the point is in some way controversial. These are the times when reasoning has a contribution to make.

As soon as we start to present reasons, to argue in words, then, we are acknowledging that the point we are driving toward is *not* self-evident, that it *is* controversial, that everyone may not agree with us. That is why it is irrelevant to say in a paper, "Of course, this is only my opinion, and someone else may think differently about it." That point is assumed from the beginning of any argument. Indeed, it explains why we *must* present reasons, why the simple assertion of our opinion is not enough. No reader will attach much importance to a single opinion; on the other hand, a reasoned opinion is worth hundreds of unreasoned ones.

We also concede, in presenting reasons, that we care about the reader's opinion. We are presenting the reasons to bring about a change in that opinion, and we imply that we care enough about the opinion to try to change it. The reader's opinion matters, then, and the opinion and the reader both deserve respect. It is for this reason that grammatical errors, for example, or misleading statements, or overgeneralizations, are so disturbing—they imply that the writer does *not* respect the reader.

More than two thousand years ago, as we saw in Chapter Six, Greek philosophers identified the three major areas of life in which verbal reasoning was appropriate. In these areas, they noted, no certainty was possible. The writer (or speaker) had to take the opinions of the reader (or hearer) seriously in order to find areas of agreement from which to modify these opinions or ideas. The reader had to be respected because, at the end of the argument, actions would follow from the agreements that had been reached.

In all of these areas, as the ancient Greeks noted and as recent philosophers of language have agreed, the arguments come down to a discussion of human values. No such argument is going to be independent of the beliefs of its audience. Large changes in that audience are unlikely. The most that can be hoped for is some small movement of the reader, and that movement must be accomplished by contact of minds through a common vocabulary and familiar ways of proceeding. The aim is mental cooperation, not compulsion.

According to this view, a writer must always acknowledge that he or she does not have the final word, the authority, or the self-evident logic that would put the written words beyond question. The writer presents examples, not proofs, takes the positions of the opponent into account, and backs insight by application. These goals are a far cry from the usual view of reasoning as overpowering, smashing, steamrolling the opposition, effecting immediate and total change of view or idea.

ACTIVITY 7–5: READING FOR VALUES

How do you argue for a value? Presumably, if a value needs to be argued, it isn't generally accepted by the audience or isn't being applied in the circumstances in questions. But if the value isn't accepted, how can it be made acceptable? Aren't values the very things that prevent agreement?

Begin by looking for arguments that rest on values, or that even argue in so many words for a specific value such as charity, fairness, honesty, and so on. Editorials are good places to look; so are political essays intended to contribute to public debates. Not all such writings are effective, however, and you might have to discard several before finding one that doesn't "preach to the converted" or that simply takes its point for granted.

In small groups, try to understand how the writer argues for the value. Is the value in question linked to another, for example? Is it simply presented at length? What seems to make the presentation effective?

A FINAL NOTE ON REASONING

This is one chapter that ends really without concluding. There is a great deal more to say about reasoning. The topics we have taken up lead on to others even more interesting: Problemsolving as arguing to an agreed-on goal might lead to a study of negotiation, for example, and of the strategies whereby skilled negotiators try to reach agreement despite conflicting positions.

Problemfinding might lead to a study of advertising and a look into the relations between argument and persuasion. Studies of reasoning like mine of Orwell's and yours of a writer you chose might lead to a study of writings in which the reasoning seems to break down, perhaps resulting in what are called "fallacies."

We have said that examples can argue for a position; could the same example be used in two opposing arguments? Also, we might extend that discussion into literature to see how a novel or short story might at the same time be an argument of some kind. As we looked at arguing about values, perhaps you thought about whether men and women argue differently, whether people in other cul-

tures do, whether lawyers and doctors and engineers argue differently about the values of their professions.

There are also many interesting questions about how *readers*
respond to arguments. If a truth really is self-evident, does it need
to be stated? How much of an argument can be left out for readers
to supply?

Reasoning is one area in which we can confidently expect to
go on learning and improving all during our lifetimes. Near the end
of such a lifetime, we hope, awaits something like wisdom, which
we might describe here as knowing what kinds of arguments really
tell and what kind don't and, in addition, of knowing which arguments lead to results that really stand up to the passage of time. We
all must remain open to growth and development in regard to
reasoning.

CHAPTER 8

How People Structure and Organize

THE POINT OF THIS CHAPTER

The point of this chapter is to give you the opportunity to think about the structure of writing. By *structure*, I mean any characteristic of words that isn't merely sequential—the result of one word's following another—but that links words that aren't next to each other. You already use structure in your verbal communications; you use it unconsciously when you tell a story and give it a beginning, a middle, and an end. This chapter is designed to help you think about structure more consciously and more deliberately.

IS STRUCTURE A CONTAINER?

When we think of writing an essay, we often think of writing to fit a particular structure. It is worth noting that the word "essay" was first used in the sixteenth century and meant a "try," an attempt, a kind of writing much less structured than the kinds that were around at that time.

The structures we associate with the essay nowadays are in fact later inventions. At some point, someone found a particularly simple or effective way of performing some particular writing task, and, by ignoring the content, produced a shell, an empty form into which other ideas could be squeezed.

It is possible for a writer to look at structure as a container to fill, particularly if the structure is a routine one, made habitual by the practices of an office or a laboratory, as in a daily or weekly report. A regular structure or format saves time and effort because many decisions don't have to be remade each time the next report is filed ("How much do I say about such and such an incident? What details are needed in the report?"). However, even those writers who look at structure this way report that filling a structure sometimes gives them ideas. How is this possible?

It is possible, I think, because a structure is itself a kind of idea, and ideas beget ideas. Perhaps we can think of structure as the outside of an idea—no idea is complete without an inside and an outside—and when we find a form for an idea, we enable the idea to become independent of us and available to others.

Writers report that their ways of organizing material often feel like ideas, that the organizing feels as much like thinking as the generating of material that preceded it. Some will even say that a structure or an organization is something they think *with*. What they mean, apparently, is that it is also possible to allow material to generate its own structure. By contrast with the routine writing mentioned above, this kind of writing requires a new format every time—a more strenuous task but one that allows the writer more flexibility in adapting to a variety of requirements.

Another reason that writing to fill a structure can generate ideas is that constraints or limitations often help rather than hinder, strange as it may seem. The next activity is meant to illustrate this possibility.

ACTIVITY 8–1: A FEELING FOR FORM

By placing a particular limitation on your freewriting, you easily see how structure can help you write. It might take more than one try, but it is a useful exercise in its own right, as well as for the point being made here.

Try freewriting with the usual rule (keep the writing implement moving, no matter what) and add only one additional rule of form, that all words must be two syllables or less.

Many people initially groan at this restriction. Some of the loudest groaners are usually the ones who say, after a couple of tries, that not only did the restriction rapidly become second nature, but that it apparently improved their ability to say even complicated things with simplicity and elegance.

The two-syllable restriction used in the previous activity illustrates what it means to think "with" a form. The form need not be just a restriction on word choice, of course. It can be a particular kind of paragraphing (generalization and example, to choose a simply one), a particular relationship of paragraphs (such as the five-paragraph essay, which begins with a paragraph that states the main point as a three-piece divided thesis, develops each piece in a body paragraph, and then concludes with a paragraph that reassembles the pieces of the main thesis), or almost any other kind of verbal patterning at all. We'll look at paragraphs later in this chapter.

The reason these forms or structures can produce ideas, I think, is that we generally don't think we have an idea until we can communicate it to someone else (even if we aren't actually able to communicate it right away). Before arriving at this stage, we have intuitions, hunches, hints, suspicions, guesses, and a lot of other more-or-less chaotic impressions; but we know we have an idea when we have some way of representing it in words that other people can understand. When we employ only two-syllable words or use a comparison format or write a five-paragraph essay, we begin with a pattern we know other people will notice and understand, and whatever we put into the form will thus be already available. Of course, the material might not *fit* the form—that is a problem for revision. But only forms can generate ideas, and perhaps the reason is that forms are already partially ideas themselves.

Is structure a container, then? Clearly it *can* be usefully treated that way. But form doesn't *have* to be seen as separate from ideas because the connection between form and idea can be much more immediate. The idea might come with a form already built in, or the idea a writer intended to use might change to another idea when given a particular form. Form and structure are *metaphors*, after all, ways of talking about effects of words on readers, and it is no wonder that metaphors should sometimes give complicated answers.

HOW READERS SEE STRUCTURE

Even if a structure appears to be routine, it still helps readers because it gives so much important information. Even a simple structure like a beginning, middle, and end helps readers know where they are in a story. Because the structure keeps readers oriented, it gives them confidence that they are reading as the writer intended, that they are constructing meanings like the ones they were supposed to construct and anticipating things that really do show up. Readers who have a sense that the writer has an orderly plan will read on much more willingly and will retain more than readers who do not perceive a plan.

Another benefit of a clear structure is that it almost instantly becomes a familiar part of the meaning within which readers can accommodate any unfamiliar information and insights that the writer presents. Once readers recognize the form, they can take it for granted and use it as a map for the writing as a whole. More complicated structures can save time in this way. In a report, for example, some readers might not need the detailed analysis to be found in an appendix but might be willing to settle for the general overview found in an abstract or introduction; on the other hand, some might want to go directly to the appendix to examine the detailed information and ignore the more general level of argument in the body of the report.

Readers see structure in two main ways, through sequence and through relationships. Sequence allows readers to find out where they are in a piece of writing, and relationships allow them to recognize the hierarchy of the various parts, such as cause-to-effect, generalization-to-example, and so on. From these relationships, readers can construct a mental picture or map of the writing as a whole that is more efficient and easier to keep track of than a long, unrelated series of items.

Thus we can see that structure is really a way of saying two things at once, of giving better coherence and easier access to one's ideas and examples. Because clear structure can benefit readers so much, it is no wonder that most writers consider it a necessary requirement.

PARAGRAPHS AS ARGUMENTS

The *paragraph* is a prime example of a structural element that makes material more manageable because it breaks longer stretches of writing into separate chunks. In doing so, paragraphs create a need for connection among themselves. They also create a space in which a writer can treat a thought or thoughts as a single idea. The form of a paragraph says, "Consider this material as a well-developed unit, a significant step in the argument being made."

Who invented the paragraph? The idea that someone *could* invent the paragraph strikes some people as very odd. But someone must have more or less invented it, because the English paragraph as we know it, even in all its diversity, is not much more than a century old. It isn't a fact of nature. People did use indentations in prose 300 years before that, and sometimes they marked off units we could compare to modern paragraphs, but systematic paragraphing is really quite recent.

Seeing the paragraph this way makes it an instrument of expression rather than an arbitrary requirement. Paragraphs are far more flexible than people sometimes think, as we shall see, and this amounts to saying that paragraphs can be reinvented whenever necessary. Fiction writers wrestle with problems of paragraphing frequently, but even technical writers do, too, when they think, for example, about how particular kinds of readers will want to segment some complicated instructions.

ACTIVITY 8–2: WHEN IS A PARAGRAPH?

To prepare for this activity, you need to select a passage of about a page in length, 250 to 350 words. It can be from anywhere, but it will be less useful if it comes from a newspaper because newspaper paragraphs follow rather unique guidelines, than if it comes from some other printed text. Textbooks are of less use than original works in various fields, and you can contribute most to the activity if your source is somewhat unusual. Try to find such a passage that makes reasonable sense apart from its context.

Retype the passage without any paragraph breaks. Be sure to keep a copy of the original for the sake of comparison.

In class, exchange passages (or pass them around a small group). With the passages you are given, try to decide where the paragraph breaks should go, and keep track in notes of why you put them where you do.

When everyone in your group has had a chance to read and reparagraph each passage, examine your different versions. If you can, reach a consensus about where the breaks should go before the person who chose the passage presents the original. If the original is quite different from your versions, try to find some pattern or reason for the differences. You might, for example, have different ideas about how much transition is required between paragraphs. You might reasonably conclude that your group's paragraphing is superior to the original, at least for you as readers.

Paragraphs vary not only in the way they break apart the larger flow of material and argument but also in the way they are arranged internally. The metaphor of structure that we discussed in Chapter Three is also helpful in discussing this kind of internal arrangement. A common paragraph structure is supposed to be a main idea, stated, then restricted or narrowed, then illustrated, and then summarized. This is called a T-R-I paragraph, for topic-restriction-illustration. In many paragraphs, there are two levels of approach, one more general or abstract and one more specific or concrete; these two levels can interweave, or one can precede the other in a structure looser than the T-R-I kind.

ACTIVITY 8–3: ANTHOLOGY OF PARAGRAPHS

Take one of the paragraphs from your source, retype it onto a clean page, and make copies for everyone in your group. Give each person a complete set from the whole group, an anthology of paragraphs.

Once you have your paragraph anthology, sort the paragraphs by their structures into the types that seem to you most distinct. One way to begin is to study one carefully, then compare it with a second. Look for all possible differences. Then compare these two with a third—is it more like the first or the second?

How many types do you see, and how would you label their differences? Can you see why the different types might have been invented? Does your classification "leak," or does it sort clearly? Can you define the central concept of "paragraph" from your approach, or is the variety too overwhelming?

When we look at the external structure of paragraphs, we often come to see paragraphs as units in an argument. When we look at their internal structure, we often come to see them as flexible instruments of composition, shaped by their function in the larger structure of the essay or other writing.

PARAGRAPHS AS PUNCTUATION

Just like capital letters and periods, some paragraphs begin and end larger units—in this case, a chapter, a book, or perhaps merely an argument within a larger unit. The paragraphs that do these jobs are often different from the paragraphs that carry the main thread of the writing, as you will see when you examine some examples in the next activity, which deals with common ways of writing opening and concluding paragraphs.

ACTIVITY 8–4: BEGINNINGS AND ENDINGS

Half the class should collect an anthology of opening paragraphs (from essays or, if possible, from a wider range of writing types), and half should collect concluding paragraphs. Compared with your results from Activity 8–3, what special features seem to characterize these beginnings and endings? Could you give a list of five favorite opening strategies, or five endings? Could you specify in more detail what must happen in each location?

FORMATS

In almost every form of life, there are accepted ways of doing things. These patterns and routines save time by serving as agreements about how things should be done. They function both as guides and as standards against which performance can be measured.

In many jobs, professions, hobbies, and activities, there are expected ways of writing. A police report, a legal brief, a business report, an obituary—each has its own independent requirements that must be met by anyone who wants to be successful in the field. Each is designed to work in a certain way with certain kinds of readers who will do predictable things with it.

Despite the enormous variety of such formats (by "format" I mean a structure that is required, official, or habitual), some common principles give most of them their different shapes. At the most general level, these principles require the writing to be adapted to the audience's expectations. The next activity is meant to focus on more specific principles of format design. Why is each as it is?

ACTIVITY 8–5: THE PRINCIPLES OF FORMATS

Procedure

Each small group in the class should make itself responsible for a different format. Some with scientific interests might study the formats of scientific reports in different fields, while those with business interests might concentrate on the annual report, the business report, the bad-news letter, or some other type of interest. One group should study the five-paragraph essay and the essay examination. Still others might want to investigate formats especially suited for a specific field or even a specific profession or business. One might want to look at how résumés vary from field to field.

In each group, focus on the large units of the writing, the parts just smaller than the whole. You could imagine that you have invented this format, or you could talk to someone who uses it all the time. Why is it designed the way it is? What are its advantages? Does it have drawbacks? For example, the business report is designed to be read by several different groups of readers, each needing a different level of detail; hence the abstract, the main report, and the appendices. But the wide variety of audiences that might read a given report can easily lead to empty verbiage.

Discussion

When the group reconvenes, try to find the principles behind the formats, since these principles should help you prepare to write the new formats you will meet in the future. Does it seem to be a general principle, for example, that all formats have some type of introduction that in some way stands apart from the main business and leads into it gradually, or are there cases when a format begins it main job directly? And if you choose the second of those alternatives, when do you find introductions and when don't you? You can ask similar questions of the elements of any format.

A FINAL NOTE: THE IMPORTANCE OF STRUCTURE

There are hundreds of formats that we can follow in writing prose, even if we narrow our attention to a single type like "business report" or "sales letter." Each is a whole in which the parts affect each other rather than merely a series of items linked one after another. In a series or list, the connection between any two parts is just, "Here's another. . . ." But in other structures, the implied announcement may be "Here is the significance of what you have just read," or "Here is the supporting detail for what you have just read," or "Here are the procedures by which you can arrive at the same results we did." The variety of possible connections generates the variety of possible formats.

These connections make particular meanings, and we could say then that format or structure is a kind of meaning, too. Structure gives a reader something to *do* with the material being presented, some way to locate it and attach it to what's around it. And structure as a whole, of course, sends a message as well: "This material has been arranged in a deliberate plan so that it is easier to take in" or ". . . so it reveals an underlying cause" or ". . . so it builds toward a strong point," or ". . . so it leads to a generalization about the data," or many others. Different parts of the structure can be addressed to different readers; perhaps a quick summary is available in one place, detailed analysis in another. Structure also breaks material apart for easier reading and makes connections explicit for easier remembering. Structure helps establish proportion: one point is given a more prominent position and gets more words than another, less important part. All these messages are conveyed by the structure of a piece of writing.

CHAPTER 9

How People Manage Sentences and Words

THE POINT OF THIS CHAPTER

When we write, we often feel that we are really wrestling with words, even though we know that those words make up sentences, paragraphs, and larger units. It is word by word that we make meaning as we write. This feeling of wrestling with words comes as we read, also, particularly if the words are difficult for us. So we might well conclude that a direct study of words is the way to improve our reading and writing.

But words don't occur in isolation. They seem always to be in sentences or sentence-like units, and even those sentences rarely occur alone, self-sufficient and able to carry someone's meaning adequately. As writers, we must take account of this fact: Words occur in sentences and larger units and improving as writers means improving our use of words *within* these larger structures.

Sentences have been a standard part of writing instruction for a long time. Most of the grammar we learn in school involves sentence structure, with subjects and predicates, adjective clauses and adverbials, restrictive and nonrestrictive modifiers, and lots more of that sort of technical terminology. The terminology has a place, of course, and so does grammatical study (see Chapter Ten for more on grammar and usage).

We can study words and sentences in the most minute grammatical detail and learn interesting things about how they work. This chapter, however, suggests a kind of overview for sentences and words, a framework within which you can continue your own investigations for years as you read and write in college and after. The framework is a simple one: It presents sentence boundaries and word choice as flexible and related to questions of audience.

SENTENCES

The most common definition of a sentence—that it is "a complete thought"—is one of the least helpful for most writers because it wasn't developed for writers at all. It was developed for grammarians, who mean by "complete" that all the required *grammatical* parts are there. But since grammatical concerns rarely enter our minds as we write, the grammatical completeness of a sentence isn't something we consider very often (except in proofreading, of course).

Some other unhelpful definitions come from linguistics, the scientific study of language. If you are a linguist and your job is to analyze a text in some language or other, you naturally want to take the text apart into manageable units, and sentences are available to help you do that. So you can define a sentence as something that begins with a capital letter and ends with a period. But people who aren't doing linguistics won't get much out of that definition either. A better linguistic definition talks about the function of the thing punctuated with a capital letter and a period, but again, the general function doesn't give writers enough to work with. So writers generally develop their own notions about sentences and sometimes are quite content to leave these notions unformulated and intuitive.

Intuitions can be guided, however, and that is the point of the activities in this section. The next activity is specifically designed to help you develop a way of thinking about sentences that makes sense to you as a writer.

ACTIVITY 9–1: HOW SENTENCES ARE MADE

Procedure

To begin this activity, you need a newspaper article of a few paragraphs or more. You are to take it apart into the simplest sentences you can, preserving the meaning of the original as best you can.

Suppose the original articles goes like this:

> Robert Grady, owner of "The Office" bar and restaurant in Orlando, has learned what it's like to fight with Coca-Cola. Sued by the huge soft-drink company last year after customers at his establishment had been served Pepsi when they had asked for Coke, Mr. Grady wanted to fight in court.
>
> But some of Mr. Grady's customers were investigators for Coca-Cola, paid to check on claims that customers who asked for "Coke" have received something else and not been told.

Here is one way to rewrite the article in the simplest possible sentences:

1. Robert Grady owns "The Office."
2. "The Office" is a bar and restaurant.
3. "The Office" is in Orlando.
4. Robert Grady has learned something.
5. He has fought with Coca-Cola.
6. Coca-Cola sued Mr. Grady last year.
7. Coca-Cola is a huge soft-drink company.
8. Mr. Grady's customers were served Pepsi.
9. They had asked for Coke.
10. Some customers were investigators for Coca-Cola.
11. The investigators checked on claims.
12. Customers claimed they asked for Coke.
13. They received something else.
14. They weren't told.

Some of these sentences could be made simpler yet, but it should already be clear that the opening sentences of a newspaper article have a lot of information to convey. The reason seems to be that the basic facts need to be presented quickly so that the usual reader of a newspaper can get the information as rapidly as possible in overview, then read on for more details if desired. Because the speed of reading is so important, the writing is compressed.

When you have made a list of ten to fifteen simple sentences, exchange it with someone in your class. (Keep the original article so that the other person will have something to compare with when finished.) Now your task is to reassemble, or recombine, the other person's simple sentences into sentences that could come from the beginning of a newspaper article.

The crucial step in this activity is to compare what you reassembled with the original. Don't assume that you made a mistake just because your assembled version doesn't match the original. Chances are there were reasons for what you did as well as reasons for what the original did, and the trick of comparison here is to try to identify those reasons.

Discussion

Some of your differences will be very minor—if you had reassembled my fourteen sentences, you wouldn't have had any way to guess that the original said "owner of" rather than "the owner of," and the difference isn't great. But you also wouldn't have been able to get to "what it is like to fight with Coca-Cola" because my simple sentences didn't reproduce that part. Nor did I say twice that Mr. Grady both fought with Coke and wanted to fight in court, because there was no reason to do so in the sequence of simpler sentences.

My comparison shows that paragraphs and more complicated sentences aren't just put together out of simpler ones. Things happen in longer sentences that can't happen in shorter ones, and also things happen in paragraphs of long sentences that don't need to happen in paragraphs of shorter ones. What other general statements can you make based on your comparison that would help you manage sentences? Do you see reasons for shorter sentences, for instance?

A more complicated question you can ask when you have looked at the original article disassembled and partly reassembled, is why it looks as it does. How did the newspaper writer know where to stop the first sentence? Is all the important information in that sentence? Is some saved for a second sentence? (Perhaps you know the newspaper writer's guide of "Who, What, Where, When,

How, and Why.") Is the writer's principle really to get as much information into one sentence as possible or is there some more complicated principle at work?

After this activity of disassembling and reassembling sentences, if someone asks, "Well, what *is* a sentence, anyway?" you will realize that the answer is not so simple as "a complete thought." Sentences of some length may contain many pieces of information that could have been written as separate sentences, as "complete thoughts." So it isn't the completeness of the thought that determines where a writer decides to put the sentence boundaries. If you write something as a sentence, you say to a reader, *"This* is a unit, one section of what I'm trying to present, and I want you to *treat* this as a unit, complete in itself and just as important as the complete units or sentences around it." In other words, the way writers arrange their thoughts in sentences to some extent indicates the importance they attach to certain ideas in relation to others. In response, readers (probably more or less instinctively) attach importance to ideas as the sentence boundaries guide them.

The next activity is meant to make this point backwards, or from the inside out, while at the same time giving your sentence-making capacity a workout.

ACTIVITY 9–2: STRETCHING

Long sentences are unusual in modern English. We tend to average fewer than thirty words in each one. When we go past that length, readers may complain, because their short-term memory can't hold so much and they have to perform an extra "assembly" operation for the chunks of the full sentence that they take in during successive slices of short-term memory. (Could you feel that sentence stretching?). Still, sentences can go on successfully for ten or twenty times that easy length if they are carefully built.

That is the invitation here, to find out what means you can use to build a sentence that is 750 words long or so.

You can make the sentence out of any content you choose; a textbook might supply you with material, or a newspaper article.

You might settle for the simplest of connectives, a child's "and then," "and then," and so on, or you might find some more complicated means of connecting.

The point, again, is not that long sentences are good in themselves. The point is rather to see what devices of the language you turn to first in extending the length of a sentence and then to notice how other people have extended theirs. Some famous examples can be found easily enough: "When in the course of human events it becomes necessary for one people . . . ." The Declaration of Independence contains several very lengthy sentences, one built around a "When . . . then . . ." structure and another built around a long list of grievances against the British government.

The length of the 750-word sentence is meant to illustrate another principle as well, which is that exaggeration is a good way to learn. This principle will appear again in Chapter Ten, which takes up grammar and usage.

In disassembling sentences and then reassembling them and in building an extra-long sentence, you can become more aware of the ways you control the boundaries of sentences. You choose the length and the content of sentences in accordance with some intuitions about what you want to say and how you want to say it. These intuitions are no doubt quite different for speaking and writing, yet the basic processes are probably fairly similar. Sentences can be combined with other sentences by words like *and* and *or, but* and *not, then* and *when* or in other ways as well. Sentences will be heard or read by people who can take in only so many words at a time, who are or are not familiar with what you are talking about. In Chapter Eleven, on style, you can look in more detail at the ways you already know to do these things.

The important point about combining sentences or taking them apart is that better writing will result from making better choices. A famous example concerns what is called "sentence variety." It's a good idea, writers are often told, not to write the same kind of sentence over and over in a row. (Subject, verb, object. Subject, verb, object. Subject, verb, object.) The reason usually given is that readers get bored.

The real reasons are more complex. For one thing, writing the *same* structure over and over is a way of gaining *emphasis*, and *repeating* emphasis *too much* eventually *numbs* the reader to *all* emphasis. Like that. But repeating the same structure should be part of the repertoire of any writer for the purpose of emphasis.

Another reason for varying sentences is that sentence structure varies anyway with the job the sentence is doing. The first sentence in a paragraph is often short because its job is to introduce a new thought, and the introduction needs to give readers a quick way to handle what is coming. Later sentences, which perhaps contain lists of supporting information, could be much longer because the reader won't have to work through them but can simply take them as filling in already expected information. A final sentence could be short, to sum up or link to the next paragraph. A writer who always writes sentences of the same kind and same length is missing out on a resource of the language, then, and is ignoring the way sentences function in larger units. Such a writer keeps doing the same job over and over again, making a kind of list of sentences rather than a paragraph.

So better advice for a writer would be, "Adapt the length of your sentences to what you are saying and to the structures and units you're using to say it." You can do that if you realize that sentence boundaries are flexible and under your control.

As the next activity shows, not only sentence boundaries but also the internal workings of sentences can be controlled if you choose to pay attention to them.

ACTIVITY 9–3: COMPOSING SENTENCES

For this exercise, you can work with a picture, even a postcard, or a window with a view. You will get your content from the scene and choose your sentence form to fit it in some way.

The task is to write a single sentence, correct in its mechanical workings, the structure of which in some way represents the content.

Example

Suppose you are describing a postcard. The riverbank scene on the card shows a huge tree in the middle, from top to bottom, dividing the scene into a left half and a right half. Behind the tree is the river, which divides the scene into a top half and a bottom

half. In the shade of the tree, on the near bank of the river, fifty or
sixty people are doing a variety of things, talking, sitting, exchang-
ing goods, washing clothes, and so on.

You decide to focus on the two divisions in the scene by
writing a sentence in two complete parts separated by a semicolon.
In one part, you write about the tree and the division it makes; in
the other, you write about the river and the division it makes. Your
first draft reads:

> "The people on this side of the river sit and talk, or wash
> clothes, or buy and sell, their lives ending at the river that
> divides them from other people; the tree itself, though it
> divides the picture, makes no division among them but shades
> young and old, rich and poor, clean and dirty."

You have decided on a two-part sentence to mirror the two parts of
the scene, and in revising you can sharpen your observations
further.

The resources of the sentence are infinite. Each time we put
together a subject and a predicate, we are saying something at least
slightly different from anything said before, and we do so without
much hesitation most of the time. We have an innate capacity for
composing sentences, which is really beyond the descriptive power
of our grammars to explain. If we look at sentences in this light, we
can see in them what we see in so many other aspects of language,
the extraordinary richness of our equipment. Trying to "train"
writers in the use of this equipment seems futile because there are
so many things it can do; as writers we must learn to explore or
experiment or examine what we can do in small ways that we can
manage.

WORDS

One myth about words that seems to have weakened its hold on
people in the last few years is the notion that a big vocabulary
automatically means a better argument or suggests a smarter writer.
The best salesmen, research shows, are not the ones with big
vocabularies; in fact, their vocabularies are smaller than average,

but they use the words they do know quite effectively. So it is with almost everyone: knowing just the right word is nice, but it's better to use two or three for the meaning you want than to get the wrong one. Acquiring new words just for the sake of acquiring them leads to a kind of "thesaurus prose," in which fancier words are selected over simple ones that could exactly paraphrase them. Most readers resent this prose because they find it "stuck up," pretentious, and wasteful. It is better to use the words we already possess in more and more careful ways and to allow new words into our vocabulary only when they are necessary for a specific meaning or purpose.

To get a sense of the richness of our everyday vocabulary, the following activity removes it from its context and lets you create a new setting for it.

ACTIVITY 9–4: DESIGNING WORDS

Discussion

Walter Erickson, the Canadian architect who designed Simon Fraser University in British, Columbia, would teach only first-year students. His first assignment was always the same: "Bring in seven stones." He gave his students three weeks.

Erickson's idea was that his first-year students could see things clearly, without the preconceptions or prejudices that specialized study might have given them. They would design arrangements of the seven stones that would reveal all the design principles to be found in the textbooks.

Perhaps some of his students did just go out at random and pick up the first seven stones they saw and carry them back to class to dump on the desk. But on one occasion Erickson teased a student for not suiting his clothes to the arrangement of stones he brought in. Why? Erickson's point seems to have been that design principles applied in more ways that the students thought. The students didn't have to stop with the stones themselves or observe conventional limits of assignments but were responsible for setting the limits themselves.

Another student took one stone from a deep-sea dive, one from a mountain top, and so on. Others chose by shape, by color, by chemical composition, by fracture plane, by value, by use, by density, and so on. Some went on to design their way of presenting the stones as well—two-dimensional or three, shown in slides, used in model buildings, worn on the person, and so on.

Procedure

What happens when you try to do such a design project with seven words? That is the first step of this activity: Bring in seven words that you have "designed" in some way.

There are many simple principles that you might think of right away. You could choose seven words that all begin with the same letter or that rhyme. Perhaps you like four-letter words with silent *e*'s. Maybe you like the variety of words we have for falling in love, getting drunk, insulting someone. Maybe instead of aggressive words you like words for fundamental realities. Maybe you like prepositions. Maybe you like seven words that could fit together in a variety of different sentences. Maybe you want seven words that describe someone or that tell a (very) short story. Maybe you want the seven words to occur in some larger stretch of language. Maybe you like words that read the same forwards and backwards. Undoubtedly you can think of other principles of arrangement as well.

Just as interesting as deciding how you will craft your own seven words is seeing how others have crafted theirs. Keep track of the principles people have used.

The most useful part of this activity seems to be classifying the principles people use to make words work in a design of some kind. Some people use sentences of various kinds, while other do not. For those who do not, what kinds of arrangements have you found?

This activity draws on some basic mysteries about words. How do words connect with other words? What kinds of relationships can we see? How many relationships can we manage? In a very different way, the study of literature examines these questions, too: The achievements of great poets and novelists seem to go beyond the stories they tell, their ear for dialogue, the memorable characters, the striking images and pictures they give us. By working with design principles at more than one level, the great artists seem to create in language new kinds of realities that help us see better the realities we live among every day. Words, even when isolated in an activity like the seven-words design, seem to have this power of creating a view of things, a way of looking or perceiving. I think this power of words is part of the reason people go on reading literature long after they leave school or come back to it later in life.

As writers, we can see that many of the principles used in designing sets of words are ones that we can employ as we try to craft better sentences and paragraphs. Like poets, we probably want to write economically (and the seven-word exercise makes every word count). Perhaps we want our writing to be memorable; we might not use rhyme and meter, but developing an ear for smooth ways of saying things is even more useful to people who write on the job.

Even linking by sound can be an effective principle. I remember a workshop I once attended in which a teacher was helping students prepare for essay exams. The key, he told them, lay in the four words "point-plan-paragraph-proofread." Just having each of his key words begin with the same letter made his presentation easier for them to remember.

Another common principle involves "tone" or "atmosphere." Perhaps you chose seven words that all had pleasant associations for you. A writer who used those words would have a good chance of getting you to read on and would give you a mental image of a writer very much like you.

People are generally astonished at the number of design principles they can observe through the word design activity. Yet they also recognize that most of these principles operate in everyday language. The conclusion seems inescapable: Word choice is an extremely complicated activity. Much of it goes on out of sight, unnoticed; how could we pay attention to all that complexity? Consciously we don't, probably, but we are sensitive to many shades of meaning in the words we hear and use. Perhaps this is why revising is so important—it is hard to choose words that will reveal on a page just the things we want them to and not other things we didn't mean.

PRECISION IN VOCABULARY

In this section, my goal is to give you a chance to examine the matter of *precision* in writing. What does it mean to choose or use words "carefully" or "precisely"? What are the limits of precision?

In early chapters of this book a number of activities dealt with language that was more or less automatic—the National Anthem and Pledge of Allegiance, prayers, clichés, and so on. My implication was that such automatic uses work against real learning, real reading, real writing. But there are uses for the automatic side of language. One might be to help us deal with the complexities of word choice; if we had to stop and think about all the possible principles that might help us choose the next word we spoke, we'd never get anything said.

We might also say that matters of grammar and usage should be automatic; getting them to be at least habitual is of course the point of doing drills on "its-it's" or "lie-lay" or subject-verb agreement. Still another area in which automatic language can be useful is technical vocabularies.

I use the word "automatic," in fact, because a student wrote once about the technical vocabulary he had to learn to use in piloting a plane. When a pilot approaches a landing field or wants to get weather information, much information has to be transmitted in seconds, and a coded shorthand has to be second nature to both pilot and controller. The metaphor of the "automatic pilot" of an airplane gives us a way of talking about what he meant.

Technical vocabularies are closely related to clichés, of course, in some ways. They are shortened ways of saying a great deal or of referring to a number of experiences or experiments or arguments in a single word or phrase. They also separate the expert from the beginner, so that learning them is connected with advancing in the field. Every profession seems to have some of these agreed-on and exactly understood terms. For many people, a technical vocabulary represents extreme precision, in such fields as medicine, law, accounting, and various forms of engineering.

ACTIVITY 9–5: USING TECHNICAL VOCABULARIES

If you already know a technical vocabulary that most of the members of your class do not, draw up a list of the five or seven most basic key terms someone would need to know to function in the world of that vocabulary. Perhaps you know something about nursing, or fast-food outlets, or motors, or a hobby or craft, enough anyway to give others a taste of the vocabulary. In presenting definitions of these terms, try to connect them both to everyday experiences or words *and* to the special experiences of the area in which they operate. If you can, write about why these terms are (or are not) essential: Do they make for better understanding? Do they mystify outsiders? What else might they do?

If you do not want to work with a technical vocabulary you already know or if you think you don't know one (you probably do, though!), you can interview someone in a field you'd like to know more about and ask for the five or seven key terms and their definitions. Try again to get both connections to ordinary vocabulary *and* references to the special facts of the field, and try to find out if these terms are necessities or just conveniences.

What gives a special vocabulary its power is not merely that outsiders don't know it. Every kind of job, every hobby, every game, maybe every family or group of friends develops its own shorthand ways of saying things so that the insiders' words carry information to other insiders faster than they otherwise would.

More than this, many jobs, fields, laboratories, businesses, professions, and forms of recreation have their own ways of looking at the world, their own logics, their own ways of finding out new things, their own "research and development" and ways of explaining and expressing things. The vocabulary of a field works within this "small world" as part of its larger efforts, and mastering the vocabulary is part of mastering that slice of life.

An interesting question is whether these different areas of our lives can be translated for each other; I know of controversies but no definitive answers to this question. Vocabularies are interesting because they are one of the ways in which we can see the differences.

One way to look at what writers do is to see that any piece of writing develops as it goes along a particular vocabulary for dealing with a certain kind of experience. Anyone who has ever written directions understands how this works. If you try to write for someone else just how you make a paper airplane, for example, you will quickly find out that you need to be able to specify in exact detail just where the folds are to be made. You will almost certainly take some existing words and make technical terms out of them, words like "fold in half" and "fold down" and "turn" and "open," specifying the first time you use them (and perhaps using pictures) just what you have in mind. Following someone's directions, or reading in general, is learning how to apply these terms to the task or the experience being discussed and to future occasions of these as well.

Technical vocabularies seem to me to fit together two important varieties of language, the automatic and the considered. The automatic part of them comes from the desire for efficiency, while the considered side comes from the desire for accuracy. These two might be seen as pressures pushing on the vocabulary, trying to make it both more efficient and more accurate all the time, and, as they do that, of course, the technical vocabulary gets farther and farther from the ordinary uses of the words. Then the technical terms get out of reach of a general public, and explanations are necessary. These are natural processes, which it is good to be aware of.

CONCLUDING ACTIVITY: REVISING WORDS AND SENTENCES

This is a different kind of revision exercise. It asks you to measure your writing along a couple of dimensions and then make some changes. These kinds of measurements can be made by computer, and you can find this sort of revision guide in many of the advanced word-processing programs on the market. The question is, what can these kinds of revision do and what can they not do?

Procedure

Choose a passage of your own writing of approximately 100 words in length, selecting the end at the end of the sentence that is nearest to the 100-word mark. Count the sentences. Count the total number of words. Count also the words of three syllables or more (not including proper names or words that get their third syllable from suffixes like *-ed* or *-es*).

Insert these counts in the following formula (see example below):

0.4 (total words/sentences
+ (100 × three-syllable words)/total words)

Calculate the "readability" of your passage by doing the arithmetic. You will get a "grade level": 10 is grade 10, 14 is second year in college, and so on.

If the readability of your sample is below 12, try to raise it by revising the passage to make longer sentences, use longer words, and so on. If the readability is above 12, try to reduce it by shortening sentences and words.

Example

Here is a passage of 100 words or so:

> Herbal preparations, long a part of folk medicine, are sometimes praised as "natural" remedies, and their use is often promoted by the idea that they produce a more natural sleep than medicines created artificially in a chemistry laboratory. These opinions are based more on wishful thinking than on well-founded scientific arguments. We should keep in mind when dealing with such questions that substances of plant origin do not necessarily produce only beneficial effects. They can also have dangerous side-effects, and various examples, such as the carcinogenic effect of nicotine in tobacco, are familiar enough. The documentation of how these herbal substances work should therefore be based on scientific investigations that are as rigorous as those required for synthetic drugs.

From *Secrets of Sleep*, Alexander A. Borbely, (New York: Basic Books, 1986) 85–86.

Word Length: 119. (I kept the last sentence so the passage would make better sense.)

Number of sentences: 5.

Three-syllable words: preparations, medicine, natural, remedies, idea, natural, medicines, artificially, chemistry, laboratory, opinions, scientific, arguments, origin, necessarily, beneficial, dangerous, various, examples, carcinogenic, nicotine, tobacco, familiar, documentation, scientific, investigations, rigorous, synthetic = 28. (This count is an attempt to identify hard words; the argument is that, even though some of these words are easy, those will be balanced by some two-syllable words that are harder.)

Formula:

1. total words/sentences = 119/5 = 23.8
2. 100 × 28 three-syllable words = 2800

3. (100 × 28 three-syllable words)/total words = 2800/119 = 23.5
4. add (1) and (3) = 47.3
5. 0.4 × 47.3 = 18.9 (appropriate reading for someone nearly through the second year of graduate school).

Discussion

The measurement of readability is controversial, of course. Some reading specialists think the available formulas, especially the one I give here, are far too crude. But I present it because it is available on computers, because versions of it have been written into some states' plain-English laws, and also because I think it can be helpful if used with some caution. In the sample passage, for instance, I think the mechanical measurement of difficulty gives a result that is much too high. I think most college freshmen can read the passage easily and understand it, even out of its context. So the question becomes, what has the writer done to make his material easy to read?

For one thing, he twice connects clauses with "and," the very easiest connective. He uses what are called *resumptive modifiers*, so that "these opinions" and "such questions" tell us precisely what a sentence is referring to in the previous sentence. And he reuses some of the longer words he has introduced, such as "natural," "scientific," and "medicine." (Nor is that all, as careful reading will show.)

If we were to revise the example only slightly, making breaks where the author made connectives and changing or omitting a few words, we could reduce the readability score significantly, of course:

Herbal preparations, long a part of folk medicine, are sometimes praised as "natural" remedies. Their use is often promoted by the idea that they produce a more natural sleep than medicines created in a lab. These opinions are based more on wishful thinking than on well-founded scientific arguments. We should keep in mind when dealing with such questions that substances of plant origin may not have only good effects. They can also have harmful side-effects. Examples such as the effect of nicotine in tobacco are well known. The account of how these herbal substances work should therefore be based on scientific tests that are as strict as those required for synthetic drugs.

A new calculation now shows a readability of

$$0.4 \ (114/7 + 100 \times 16/114) \qquad = 0.4 \ (16.3 + 14) = 12.1$$

This drastic drop indicates that the difficulty was indeed a matter of only a few words and connectives and that the formula much overstated the difficulty of the original (and does not indicate the somewhat childish sound of the revision).

The point of revising and remeasuring in this way is to focus attention of some of the more obvious characteristics of sentences and words to see what can be learned from them. Obviously no mechanical formula is going to assess difficulty of a text reliably because the difficulty depends on subject matter and audience as well as on the things a computer can count. But this kind of crude measuring can occasionally identify problem areas or strengths. If readers complain about the difficulty of a text, and if its words and sentences satisfy the formula for easy readability, then the problem is elsewhere, presumably in an area in need of more drastic revision.

PART FOUR

IMPROVING
YOUR WRITING

In Chapters Ten through Thirteen, you will be working with the details of language in an attempt to improve your writing in general. As you work through these chapters, you should be polishing at least one of your earlier drafts, getting it ready for submission or publication.

CHAPTER 10

The Glamor
of Grammar

THE POINT OF THIS CHAPTER

For generations people have believed that learning grammar was a good way to learn to write. But recent research has shown conclusively that learning the grammar we have available in schoolbooks today does not improve writing, does not even improve our ability merely to write without grammatical errors. Yet we continue to believe that grammatical information must be of some use, and we all know that writing is evaluated partly by its correctness, by whether it matches the grammatical standards of its readers.

Here we have an obstacle facing us as writers. One of the criteria writers must face is grammatical correctness, but we don't yet know how to make it directly teachable or learnable. We *must* learn it, but no one can teach it to us.

How are we to meet the standard? How are we to account for the generations of mistaken belief, or was it mistaken? Is there some problem with the particular grammar we have been trying to

use? This chapter tries to help you find some connections between
your writing and (some version of) grammar.

THE PARTS OF SPEECH

In his autobiography, *Personal Memoirs*, which he finished a
few days before his death in 1885, Ulysses S. Grant wrote that he
had heard 'A noun is the name of a thing' repeated so often that
eventually he believed it. Repetition is the way most grammatical
information is taught and learned, even though for many people
rote and repetition are the most painful ways of learning anything.
It is probably no wonder that grammar is one of the most resented
areas of instruction.

Even so, grammatical ideas have a peculiar hold on us. Grant
went on, "I think I am a verb instead of a personal pronoun. A verb
is anything that signifies to be; to do; or to suffer. I signify all three."
He was dying of throat cancer, in great pain and no little disgrace
thanks to enormous debts and political scandal, desperate to recoup
enough money through the sales of his autobiography to support his
large family after he was gone. Odd that parts of speech should have
occurred to him at such a time.

Parts of speech rarely attain for us such importance as they had
for Grant or for the medieval philosophers who thought that
different kinds of words referred to different "modes of being" in
the world. For them, nouns signified the kind of being that physical
objects have ("this tree"), verbs corresponded to the kind of
existence that actions and events have ("raining" or "grows"),
adjectives to qualities like color, and so on. What kind of existence
corresponded to prepositions, or articles? No doubt there were
people who thought they could find out about the world by asking
such questions about words.

Just as we might disagree with those philosophers, we might
disagree with the idea that there is anything glamorous about
grammar, about parts of speech, about the uses of words in sentences, about diagramming sentences, or about the myriad rules of
good usage. We have a similarly unpleasant view of glamor sometimes—that it is superficial, just fashion, fads.

So it might come as a surprise to hear that both words originally
meant something more significant; perhaps even more surprising is
that the two words were originally connected. In a famous observation by Jacqueline de Romilly in *Magic and Rhetoric in Ancient
Greece*, the origins of the two are linked:

glamour and *grammar*, or, in French, *grimoire* and *grammaire* were originally the same word and thus combined, even in the vocabulary, the magical and rationalistic aspects of speech.

Both words have suffered since their separation. The original concept, we may suppose, must have referred to profound mysteries and the possibility of profound knowledge and power.

We have lost the link between the words and abandoned long ago the medieval idea about understanding the world, or the human mind, by looking only at the structures of language. However, the connections between language and the mind have in the last few decades become the focus for an entire scientific subdiscipline. Psychologists, neurophysiologists, electrical engineers, sociologists, psycholinguists, and experts in artificial intelligence have all turned their attention to verbal behavior, either in trying to understand how our minds work or in trying to develop machines to do some of the things our minds can do.

The reason they have been studying language so intensively is not hard to find. We still believe that one of the things that makes human beings human is language, that our capacity to use words makes us special and different. Inquiry into language is inquiry into our special nature and is indeed a study of profound and mysterious questions. The name for this study in general is *linguistics*, and the result of its inquiry is called *grammar*. But the grammar that it produces is not much like the traditional grammar to be found in most schoolbooks. What is it like, and how might it help writers? To begin answering this question, consider the first three stanzas of "Silent Poem" by Robert Francis:

backroad leafmold stonewall chipmunk
underbrush grapevine woodchuck shadblow

woodsmoke cowbarn honeysuckle woodpile
sawhorse backsaw outhouse wellsweep

backdoor flagstone bulkhead buttermilk
candlestick ragrug firedog brownbread

All these compound nouns name more or less familiar "country" things. I've been told that a "shadblow" is a kind of berry, a "wellsweep" is a gadget that cleans the surface of a well, a "bulkhead" is a regional word for the kind of cellar door that covers a stair coming up to ground level, and a "firedog" is another regional word for an andiron, the metal gratelike structure that supports wood in a fireplace.

One of the reasons we study literature, as I have mentioned before, is that it often shows us extreme cases or tests the frontiers of language. One frontier Francis is testing in this poem is exactly the limit in our minds that would have said you couldn't make a poem this way, out of one type of word. Don't you actually need to say things, we would have said?

Almost everyone who reads this poem would agree that it does say something, of course; more than that, we feel we could go on with the poem easily if we tried. We could draw compound nouns from our own backgrounds to name some of the important objects of our pasts. We could feel, in the compoundings, the way all of us put together out of simple words the bigger words that express our experiences. We might even see that the poem is going in a particular direction; perhaps it is the record of a trip, ending in a kitchen and a meal.

When we have seen all these things, we have seen the grammar of the poem, the way its words fit together and function (that is a traditional definition of grammar). Part of our natural language-using capacity is this ability to read a poem like Francis's and make some sense of it, and part of the task in finding a grammar we can use as writers is cleaning out the rote "learning" about grammar that clogs that capacity.

ACTIVITY 10–1: ANY ENGLISH NOUN CAN BE VERBED

Discussion

In the "sentence" activities in Chapter Nine, you saw that sentence boundaries are flexible, that writers can choose where to end one sentence and begin the next. This activity extends the same point to parts of speech. The flexibility of nouns and verbs is important because it is the foundation for advanced work in improving clarity.

(To give a hint of that advanced work, it seems that clearer writing results from putting the doers of actions into subject nouns and the actions themselves into predicate verbs; this is exactly the opposite of what much bureaucratic prose does.)

Procedure

Go to the dictionary and find ten nouns and ten verbs. Try for nouns and verbs that do not have identical counterparts as verbs and nouns; in other words, avoid words like "run," which obviously can be either. Choose instead a noun like "blackboard" or "hat." What might it mean to blackboard someone or to hat something? Put a name on the blackboard to indicate that a student has done something wrong? Catch something in a hat?

Bring your twenty words to class and exchange with a partner. With the twenty words you receive, try to concoct sentences that use the given verbs as nouns and the given nouns as verbs without changing the form of the word. Suppose your nouns include "book". Perhaps you already know that "Book him, sergeant" means to enter a suspect's name in a police register prior to detaining in jail or that "I can't go to the movies; I have to book tonight" means that someone has to read books or study for school. So you have two ways of turning this noun into a verb.

Many verbs go easily and naturally into nouns, but you might be able to find some hard ones. How about "anticipate" or "operate"?

Reflection

The point of trying to stretch your grammatical capacity in this way is to develop flexibility, to give yourself as a writer some additional options you might not have been aware you had.

What does it mean that English nouns can generally be verbed and vice versa? Just one of the things it might mean is that parts of speech aren't categories that exist in isolation. A word isn't a noun or verb until it's in a sentence, until it's used. And use, of course, is human use, use in writing and reading. As you might guess, those uses are far more complicated than can be presented to children in their beginning grammar classes.

Recent research has suggested, in fact, that parts of speech do not belong to the closed system we might have thought they did. If you were taught that there are eight parts of speech (or seven, or nine—the arbitrariness of the number is suspicious), you might well have wondered *why* there are eight. In English, it turns out, the categories are not at all as cut and dried as we sometimes suppose. The criteria by which we divide adjectives and adverbs, for example, are so complex and have so many exceptions and slippery "in-between" cases that modern functional grammarians have decided to say that there is a continuum or "gradient" between the two word classes.

Parts of speech are just the beginning of a grammar, to be sure. But modern researchers have extended their insights into all the areas of grammar, into syntax (how words fit together), semantics (what words and groups of words mean), and pragmatics (what words are used to do). In all these areas, they have brought the kind of approach that we use when we read Robert Francis's poem: they look first to see just what the language actually does and derive the grammar from function rather than preconceived categories. This functional or practical approach is yielding results, but for writers just the approach itself may be even more important than the results for some years to come because the approach is one we all can profitably take. The next section examines how we as writers can adopt an experimental and functional approach to grammar and considers what might happen if we do.

GRAMMAR FOR WRITERS

You might be surprised to hear that the grammar you learned in grade school or high school is outdated, but that is almost certainly the case. Most high school texts—*Warriner's* is perhaps the most famous—still have a heavy concentration on what is called "traditional" grammar. "Traditional" may sound good until you inquire which tradition is meant. The tradition turns out to be the tradition of Greek and Latin grammars, and since English is at bottom a Germanic rather than a Greek or Latinate language, the Greek and Latin systems don't fit it very well. To make some parallels, "traditional" medicine would mean deriving treatments from some other type of animal than man ("What works for dogs and rats will work for people!"), and "traditional" astronomy might mean continuing to assume that the earth is the center of the universe.

It is no accident that traditional grammar is generally taught by memorization. Any other learning method would invite questions that the misapplied Greek and Latin grammar would have a tough time answering. One famous example is the supposed rule against splitting infinitives in English. You aren't supposed to say "to boldly go." Instead, the purists have it, you should say "boldly to

go" or "to go boldly." Their reason turns out to be that in Greek and
Latin, you *cannot* split infinitives because they are made with
endings on the verb, so early English grammarians wishing to give
English the same prestige as Greek and Latin decided to forbid in
English what could not be done in the other languages. But there is
no reason in English for banning so-called "split" infinitives; in
fact, there is a reason to allow them.

The unfortunate result of applying Greek and Latin grammatical principles to English was that traditional grammarians attacked
a genuine communicative resource of the English language, which
allows three ways of modifying infinitives with adverbs and which
further gives a different meaning to each one. In the case of
"boldly" and "to go," two of the meanings are clearly distinct: "to
go boldly" means to go in a bold manner, while "to boldly go"
means or can mean that the going itself is a bold undertaking. There
are many other examples of Latinate rules not fitting English as
well, such as the supposed injunction against putting prepositions
at the ends of sentences ("The kind of rule up with which I will not
put," as someone wittily remarked).

The moral is clear: English grammar should be derived from
the study of English, and specifically from the study of how words
actually work as we read and write in our everyday pursuits. This
kind of study results in a *functional grammar*, and successful
writers are continually constructing their own versions of functional grammar adapted to the particular audiences and situations
in which they write.

How does a functional grammar develop, and how does one
work? One of its basic premises is that arbitrary definitions should
be avoided. You learn what nouns are by observing what they do,
not by memorizing a formula. Nouns are used to name, as the
traditional definition says, and they are also used to refer to objects,
but they have other uses as well. The job of being a noun, of course,
can be filled by a whole clause, a whole group of words with its own
internal subject and verb (as in "What I needed was more time"
where "what I needed" is a clause acting as a subject—a noun's
frequent job). Nouns can refer to agents, the doers of action, and also
(as direct objects) to things or people that are acted on. It is in referring
that nouns show some of their major functions. But that is already
more than you should accept on faith about English grammar.

Functional grammars are indeed systematic, and in more
advanced work on your writing you might well want to investigate
the systems on which grammars are now written. Short of that,

however, you can still insist that whatever *new* grammatical information you add to your repertoire of writing skills be functional.
That approach is demonstrated in the next activity.

ACTIVITY 10–2: WHAT DOES IT MEAN TO BE A PRONOUN?

Procedure

Choose a page from a paper you have written recently (you
might find it easier to work with a photocopy or even a tri-
ple-spaced, retyped version). Circle every pronoun. If you are new
to pronouns, you can circle all the personal pronouns easily
because a complete list of them is fairly short:

> I (me, my, mine); you (your, yours); he (him, his); she (her,
> hers); it (its); we (us, our, ours); they (them, their, theirs).

If you know more about pronouns, you might want to include:

> this, that, these, those, or others.

Once you have identified these words, examine carefully the
words around them to enable you to say in as much detail as
possible just what each pronoun actually does. According to traditional grammar, pronouns replace nouns or proper nouns, which is
certainly true as far as it goes. But pronouns link sentences as well
when the noun they refer to is in another sentence; this is called a
cohesive function. Pronouns do other things too. Are yours perhaps
helping you avoid repetition? Helping with the rhythm of a
sentence? Doing something else? When you finish and compare
with other people's accounts of pronouns, you have a functional
account of pronouns, of what they actually are doing for you as you
write.

Discussion

You might incidentally detect some of the common pronoun
problems—perhaps you wrote "everyone" and later replaced it
with "they" or "their." This is traditionally a no-no, since "ev-

eryone" is singular; it should be replaced with "him/his" or "her." But to avoid choosing a gender in the later pronoun, some writers have deliberately chosen to use the plural "their": "Everyone brought their favorite snack." This example may be an indication that our language is changing, and indeed languages do change over time. Not everything that was correct a hundred years ago is correct now; two hundred years ago, "ain't" was acceptable, and "aren't" in sentences like "I'm taller, aren't I?" would have been laughed at. Although "everyone . . . their" hasn't been approved by many authorities yet, it or some other item might well move from incorrect to correct in your lifetime.

Reflection

The same activity that shows how pronouns work can be turned on nouns, or adverbs, or phrases, or commas, or any traditional topic you know about and want to investigate, and, more important, it can be used to investigate any language phenomenon you notice, whether you have a name for it or not. You need observation, hypothesis, data, verification, and application to your writing to master any of them.

ERRORS

Late in the writing process, it is important to consider the possibility that we have made some errors, that we have violated standards of correctness in grammar, usage, or mechanics (these terms are not interchangeable; together they cover most of the things you can do "wrong"). How are we to eliminate these?

The short-term and long-term answers to the problem of correctness are different. The short-term answer that almost every writer uses is to get someone else to look at what you have written, particularly if you can look at something in return. This switch works because it is far easier to find errors in material you are not totally familiar with than in writing you know as well as you know something you have just written. You approach the strange writing as a reader does, and that lets you see where you are blocked or obstructed by various kinds of mechanical difficulties.

Consider the problems of sentence boundaries (the errors traditionally labeled *fragments, run-on sentences,* and *comma splices*). These three related errors cause problems for readers in

different ways. A *fragment* is part of a sentence that has been
punctuated as if it were a complete sentence. Advertisements can
be punctuated this way because the partial sentences are emphatic
and because they can be read more slowly than a complete sentence,
allowing readers to give more attention to each part. But when you
write the following, you give your readers not more time but more
trouble, because they have to guess how to reassemble the whole:

> Young entrepreneurs understand that to make money you need
> money. While others diminish their savings accounts by invest-
> ing in real estate, business, and the stock market. I intend to
> capitalize on gold and cycles.

The "while" clause could attach either to the sentence after it
or the one before, and a reader will have to spend a bit more time
and effort figuring out that it goes a bit better with the one after,
time and effort that detract from time and effort put into understanding the writer's point.

More or less opposite to fragments are *run-on sentences*, in
which the sentence boundary has been widened to include too
much rather than too little. For example,

> The price of silver climbed to ten times its original value soon
> after the price dropped down to seven dollars again.

In the paper where I read this sentence first, the context made
it clear that the price first rose, then fell, but the sentence as
punctuated says the reverse. It needs a period after "value" and a
new sentence beginning with "soon."

Like run-ons, *comma splices* join two sentences but they
include a comma to mark the fusion.

> The inflation rate climbed to 12 percent, when this occurred,
> the price of silver was five dollars and forty cents and rose to
> forty-eight dollars an ounce.
>
> Silver coins have spending value as money, they can
> always be redeemed for at least part of their cost.

Here the extra work comes from another convention about
commas, that they can indeed separate independent clauses *if* the
writer puts three together in a series: "Silver coins have spending
value as money, they can be redeemed for part of their cost, and the
investor won't be left with something completely worthless." A

reader who comes to the end of the second clause in the two examples expects to find a third. As a result, the reader has to go back to see what went wrong—did I miss a clause? Or did the writer skip one?

Dangling modifiers are another deadly error for many readers, again because they create an expectation that they then contradict.

> Living a stereotyped lifestyle, people assumed I wanted to be a nurse, a stewardess, or a teacher.

The paper from which this comes made it clear that it was the writer and not the other people who lived the stereotyped lifestyle. But, in this sentence, the opening modifier refers to the next noun, "people," so the reader must assume that the writer did not mean precisely what she said here—and this kind of assumption damages the credibility of a writer. A modifier followed by such an unexpected subject requires extra interpretive work to overcome the discrepancy, as in the other errors, and that extra effort interferes with the effort being put into comprehension.

Two other errors people often mention are *subject-verb agreement* and *pronoun reference* or *agreement problems*. By now you can probably tell how they too force readers back through a text to see what has gone wrong, how they require extra work for no return. If these or any of the seven deadly grammatical errors can be charged against you, the reason is not arbitrary. You have in fact double-crossed the very people you are trying to get to trust you, and you have gotten in your own way by sending conflicting messages to those readers.

As a reader, you can help other writers see where they have sent conflicting messages. This is, as I mentioned, the short-term solution to the problem of correctness: get other people involved. You can't see what you can't see. If you could see your error yourself, you would already be on the road to avoiding it.

The long-term answer is rather different. How are you going to improve your ability to avoid errors in the first place? Once you have found some error that needs to be eliminated from your writing, the work is only beginning.

If you ask professional writers how they learned to overcome their problems, most will tell you that simple drills didn't help much. Once in a while that is all the help a writer needs, but more often, once the writer is writing again, the error creeps back in. If you are serious about eliminating an error, you may have to engage your entire learning effort. Here is a model for how you might do that.

DESIGNING YOUR OWN DRILLS

Grammar drills have a long history, but so does the line of thought that says grammar drills, particularly mere rote ones, do not make much difference. In 1653 an Englishman named John Wallis wrote a grammar of the English language in which he tried to list the kinds of grammatical items he thought rote learning could improve. Even before that time, however, Germans named Comenius (1592–1670) and Ratke (1571–1635) had pointed out that drills by themselves were not enough because they isolated the item to be learned from meaningful discourse.

Other problems of drills have become apparent. If you work only by repairing defective examples, you might find that you remember the defects better than the remedies. You might also find that you can fix an error when you know there is one, but that you still don't get the forms correct in the first place as you write. Finally, you might develop a mental habit called a "drill set," in which you treat drills as a kind of puzzle and get the right answer as a kind of game—which apparently prevents transferring the skill you are learning into your writing.

One important observation to make before beginning work on errors is that the people who *make* the drills learn the most. This phenomenon is related to a larger one, that a good way to come to understand something thoroughly is to teach it. If you take on the task of teaching yourself, you will find that you remember much more of your practice than if you accept precooked drills from someone else.

Somehow, also, your grammatical work must start and end with words in contexts. You might recall Benjamin Franklin's reassembly of the articles he took apart—he was doing something similar. Furthermore, you should require yourself continually to focus on the functions of the items you are working with to keep out of the "drill set."

ACTIVITY 10–3: CONSTRUCTING A DRILL

Choose some grammatical or mechanical problem you would like to work on, perhaps one that has frequently been pointed out to you as a problem in your writing. Then, from the list of all possible steps, choose the ones that seem likely to make a difference to you and construct a drill package for yourself. Work your way through it, and try to decide afterward whether it has made any impact on your writing.

1. Find samples of the correct form in context.
2. Isolate the correct form and get an official explanation of how it works from a teacher, a tutor, or a handbook.
3. Find other correct forms and explain how they work to the teacher, tutor, or yourself.
4. Ask the teacher or tutor for an *incomplete* form, which they complete for you. That is, have them prepare a passage with blanks that they then fill with correct forms for you.
5. Construct an incomplete form for yourself, complete it, and then check with someone to make sure you have done it right.
6. Explain the completion you have made in (5).
7. Ask the teacher or tutor for (or find in a handbook or workbook) an incorrect example and develop an explanation of the trouble it causes (like the account above of fragments, run-ons, or comma splices).
8. Watch carefully while the teacher, tutor, or handbook fixes the incorrect example.
9. Correct an incorrect example yourself (this is the step that most people mean when they say "drill").
10. Get a detailed explanation of how the incorrect example is fixed.
11. Fix an incorrect example yourself and give a complete explanation of how you have done it.
12. Fix a series of incorrect examples, as different as possible.
13. Get from teacher, tutor, or handbook a mixture of correct and incorrect forms, select the incorrect ones, and fix them.
14. Given a passage, try to repair all the errors, including the ones you're working on.
15. Return to a piece of your own writing and proofread it for errors of all kinds, including the ones you have been practicing.

Reflection

Several steps in this long process require help from someone else, a teacher, tutor, or other authority. I want to repeat, however, that the makers of drills learn the most from them. The more you can substitute your own materials for those from a teacher or tutor, the better you will retain what you have learned.

You might be wondering at this point where the handbooks come from and how they get written. A good handbook, like a good modern dictionary, should begin with actual examples of language use. These examples should be sorted to form groups of data bearing on each specific grammatical point. Each item should be explained both in isolation and as it works in larger structures so that writers can see why it is as it is. Most handbooks fall short of this ideal, but many are starting to include functional material.

You can do a more thorough presentation of almost any grammatical or mechanical matter if you cooperate with your class on an investigation like that described in the next activity.

ACTIVITY 10–4: NATIONAL COMMA DAY

This activity could take any item of grammar or punctuation as its subject, but since commas are often a common problem, I suggest focusing on them.

Procedure

On the class day before National Comma Day, each member of the class brings two "citations" or actual examples of comma use from anywhere and writes them on a ditto master or other master copy that will be photocopied for everyone for the next class.

On National Comma Day, begin by sorting. Are the commas in the first two citations doing the same thing, or are they doing different things? Does the third citation look like the first, the second, both, or neither? Continue until you have sorted all the citations into groups.

Label the groups of citations you have made. For each group of citations, assign a group of students to formulate the principle that underlies this use of commas. Why is the comma used under these circumstances? (Why not some other mark of punctuation? Why not no mark at all?)

Each group then presents its principle and explanation to the class, which can compile a far more thorough account of commas than you can find in most handbooks.

Reflection

One important benefit of working this way is that you get a look at all the jobs a comma can do. It would be even better if you could look at all the jobs that punctuation does, as a whole, but class periods are too short. Experts agree, however, that all punctuation should ideally be seen as a complete system, not merely a collection of isolated markings.

A FINAL NOTE: GRAMMAR IN PERSPECTIVE

Writers might well not need complete grammars. They probably do need a working knowledge of sentence structures, an understanding of common errors, and most importantly a sense that grammar is a field of inquiry rather than a fixed body of doctrine. Few generalizations about words stand up to the test of a wide range of contexts because the things we do with words are so varied and so complex. Grammar might seem to offer certainties, and it certainly can offer assistance, but it cannot give the kinds of guarantees that writing teachers of old thought it could.

Grammar as I conceive of it in this chapter leads naturally to the study of style because many of the matters studied will affect the ways in which we say things. We can improve ourselves stylistically much the same as we do grammatically, by careful and sustained attention to how words actually work in sentences and paragraphs. If you are told that your sentences lack variety, you might begin a study of varying sentence structures to see when different structures are used. You might find that different kinds of sentences have different uses. You would then be on your way to making both grammatical and stylistic advance.

The ideas discussed in this chapter can also be applied to the larger subject of revision, of how you take on the task of improving a specific piece of writing. It is primarily from the experience of revising and editing that we improve as writers. This chapter has recommended ways of obtaining useful and functional information about grammar in order to revise for grammatical errors, but these recommendations can also help you revise in other areas. This chapter is meant to serve as a kind of emblem for that one.

CHAPTER 11

Style and Voice

THE POINT OF THIS CHAPTER

As readers, we picture the writer as we read. As writers, we know readers will picture us, and we try to shape the means by which readers are to infer a personality and approach.

To readers, this picture of the writer seems to be built into the words themselves. A general word for this phenomenon is *style*. Some words that apply directly to the built-in personality include *tone*, which refers to something like attitude or tone of voice, and *voice*, which refers to the distinct personality behind the writing (writing that lacks voice seems generic, impersonal, official).

STYLE AS READERS SEE IT

In Activity 9–4, which asked you to "design" seven words, you undoubtedly realized that a set of seven words could embody a number of design principles at the same time. A set could fit together as a sentence and be in alphabetical order, for example, as in "All boys can dive excellently from great heights." It would be possible to add other principles to these, such as that all words be of the same number of syllables, all be of Anglo-Saxon origin, and so on. The most noticeable "design" involves fitting words that make sense together into sentences, but readers can notice many other designs as well, and most of these fit under the general heading of "style."

One of the most noticeable patterns apart from sentence structures is probably word choice. Almost without knowing that we do it, we judge people by the words they choose—conversational or colloquial, formal, slangy, and so forth (this dimension of style is usually called *register*). Along with word choice, we may make the same judgments based on how long sentences are, how complicated their structures are, and how they fit together and refer to one another.

We judge more than register from word choice, sentence pattern, and connection. We draw conclusions also about the kind of person the writer is. We infer an attitude toward the subject and toward the readers. This set of inferences is extraordinarily important in providing a context for what we might call the "message," though it is probably more accurate to say that there would *be* no message if we couldn't perceive that the writer was like us, spoke the same language, and had similar purposes.

The study of style is no more than a study of reading, an examination of how people make sense out of a memo, a letter, some poetry, a technical manual, or other writing. It is no less than a study of reading, also, and reading can be quite complex, as we saw in Chapter Two. How can we examine such a complicated phenomenon as style?

EXAMINING STYLE

One way to examine style is to slow it down and keep track of what we are thinking as we read, focusing on perhaps a single aspect or two of what we are reading. There is more to style than this, but this kind of reading is a good starting point. Consider a short poem like this one:

Prithee, take care, that take this book in hand,

To read it well, that is, to understand.

I have remembered this poem for twenty years because it was presented to me in a special way, one word at a time, and I was invited to write after each word what I thought it meant, what the next word might be, what the word just given told me about words already read. The poem is by Ben Jonson, written almost four centuries ago, and intended to appear in the front of a book of his poems, where at first glance it probably didn't attract much attention. But reading it word by word shows that it is a well-built demonstration of its own meaning.

When I saw the first word, "prithee," I knew I was reading a request (it's an old word, made out of "pray thee," meaning something like "please" but with the sense of "pray" still there). The writer was asking the reader to do something. A request is something you make of someone who is in a position to do you a favor, to do something for you that you need done and that wouldn't get done without help. Such a request already sets up a relationship between Jonson and his intended reader, a relationship in which Jonson is politely asking for a favor of someone who is in a position to do something for him. The second word after "please" in a request, I also thought, would probably be a verb mentioning the action I should take to oblige the requester ("Please *open* this book" or "Please *tell* me what you think" or "Please *be* receptive").

The second word, "take," was indeed a verb, and so I felt I was on the right track. Jonson was asking that I please take the book, take a look at it, take time to read it, take it with me somewhere, perhaps. The next word, I thought, would tell me what I was supposed to take.

It did, but it wasn't what I had expected. Instead of mentioning something concrete that I was supposed to take, Jonson was saying "take care," be careful. The phrase makes "take" not concrete at all, but part of an idiom, maybe even a cliché, where "take" plus another word mean something entirely unlike the physical sense of taking. Who asks you to be careful besides your mother? Am I supposed to watch out for dangers in the book? Or is it "take care" in the sense of "be sure to"—take care to follow the recipe exactly, for instance? Or was it "take care *of*" something?

The next word, "that," left me mystified for a moment, I remember, until I thought of sentences like "take care that you don't fall." It seemed to be heading in the direction of a warning after all. I expected "you" or something like "take care that no harm come to you."

The second "take" made me realize I was lost. I had at this point "Prithee, take care, that take . . .". The play on the word "take" made me sure I didn't know what was going on. I had to read on for help; I had to trust Jonson to bring me out of the confusion.

When I got the rest of the first line, I found that the *second* "take" was the concrete one "take this book in hand," and the "that" was in modern English "who." Then I could see that the line asked me as a reader to be careful.

The second line, read word by word, had fewer surprises in the first half—"To read it well" is just what you'd expect a poet to ask you to do on the first page of a book of poems. But then Jonson has to explain what he's just said already quite clearly ("that is"), and he explains with the word "understand." Now it's common enough to ask to be understood, but how can we as readers be sure we have done that? We can try all we want and still not understand sometimes, read well and yet not get to what we feel the writer meant. So Jonson seems to want a little extra. We are to take care, we are to read well, and we are (somehow) to understand. Again, we are not told how that is to be accomplished; we just have to trust Jonson to lead us through to the understanding he wants. That reading on and trusting, I think, is the real favor Jonson was asking of us in this poem, and also showing us how he could lead us through to a final understanding of a poem if we just hung on.

Obviously we seldom read word by word in this way; two-line poems take an hour, a sonnet would take a week, and a memo would take a month to work out this way. We could hardly justify giving this kind of attention to any group of words unless we thought it was going to give us wisdom or insight, as literature often does. This example of the slow-reading technique isn't meant to be a model for everyday practice. But people sometimes think we shouldn't read this way because the writer didn't mean us to. I think that's wrong. I think that when we write we do control many more variables than we are aware of consciously. Consequently, if you want to understand how a writer or a piece of writing really works, give it this kind of attention. What you get is a slowed down look at how it means what it means—its style—and this can include everything that it says too.

As writers, too, we can benefit from the slow-reading method. Often we write a passage that just doesn't work. Perhaps members of our group say they don't understand it, or don't think we mean what we say, or think we are contradicting what we have said before. Often we can use this word-by-word method to track down the problem and find that we have created expectations we aren't satisfying. Perhaps we start a sentence one way and finish it another, as in "My teacher taught me the idea of eye contact in chess, which most people know little about and how it can win a game for you." The man who wrote this sentence was thinking "My teacher taught me two things—the idea of eye contact, and how it can win games." But readers pick up only the first—the idea—and think that there are two parts of the "which" structure—"which most people know little about' . . . and what? The rest of the sentence doesn't fit the expectation, and readers have to go back. To fix the problem, some sentence disassembling may be in order (see Activity 9–1, pp. 135—137).

The idea of "style" covers a lot of ground, as the example of Jonson's poem shows. Since a sense of style can so greatly enrich our sense of how we read, it is worth pursuing in its own right, as the next activity invites you to do.

ACTIVITY 11–1: READING WORD BY WORD

Choose a poem of two or three lines at most or a very short passage from a famous speech. Read it to a partner, a word or phrase at a time, while the partner writes down what the word means (paraphrase), what it adds to words already given, and what it leads the partner to expect. Have the partner read you a similar passage while you get a slowed-down look at how you actually read.

WRITING AND STYLE

If style is the effect a passage has on a reader (including what it says), writing with style is something we do whether we want to or not. Everything we write will have some style, and the writer's first problem then is to select the style that has the best chance of getting readers to do what the writer hopes they will do. A writer must also avoid making readers do things they do not want or like to do.

Improving one's style in this sense is obviously no simple business but a lifetime's work. Writers suggest that it is best begun through simplicity, by saying things directly and clearly, by learning to use the structures that readers know best and use most easily. But even that first step is difficult because nothing is harder than saying things simply. No wonder that style is a topic generally taken up in advanced writing classes.

Nevertheless, every writer can begin taking control of the style his or her words will have on the page. The shortest path at this point is to ask people, and one way to do that is with the CLOZE technique introduced in Activity 2–1. As you might remember, in a CLOZE passage, certain words are left out to see how predictable they are. The next activity asks you to use the CLOZE technique with your own writing.

ACTIVITY 11–2: CLOZE YOURSELF

Take a page or more of your recent writing, a paper you are working on for this class or some other. Leave the first sentence intact. In the second sentence and thereafter, underline every fifth word until you have underlined thirty words or so. Retype the page, leaving blanks where the underlined words were.

Give this CLOZE passage to a partner and ask to have each of the blanks filled with a single word. What does it mean if nearly every blank is filled correctly or nearly so? What does it mean if few blanks are filled? Try to fill the blanks in your partner's passage. Where you cannot fill the blank successfully, can you say what the problem is? Is it that you have no idea or that you have some idea but can't be sure which possibility is right?

READING FOR PERSONA

An important dimension of your style is who readers think you sound like. The person who is suggested by your writing is called the *persona* or *implied author*. The word *persona* means a mask, but a mask in the sense that any face is a mask. You have to have some face or other, and you have to have some persona or other too. The persona isn't you, exactly; instead, it is something you make. You can make it automatically and take what comes, but you also can begin to craft a persona and use it to help put across an idea or a point of view.

Before writing with attention to your persona, you might profitably read and notice how other writers give you a sense of who they are. What words mark them as authoritative, as angry, as concerned or intelligent or down-to-earth? Another important aspect of a persona is how noticeable it is: Does the writer seem to call attention to how things are said, or is the intent rather to make the writing itself unnoticeable? Which words, if any, call attention to how the writer writes?

ACTIVITY 11–3: READING LETTERS TO THE EDITOR

The easiest way to see personae is through contrast. Look at the letters to the editor in some newspapers. You might have to read several papers before you find two letters that differ greatly, but the more extreme your choices, the clearer will be your understanding of what contributes to each persona.

Bring your choices to a small group and read your letters aloud. Does your group notice the same features that you did? Or are there things you might be missing? (A group is a useful resource to find out how the persona of a piece of writing strikes people because a single reaction might be too eccentric.)

PERSONA AND WRITING

Considerable revision goes into adjustments of personae. Getting just the right words to create the written personality that will be most effective is not something most of us have a natural talent for. As we write more and get more responses, we can start to see words we use that help or hinder, but this too is an aspect of writing that requires continuous attention through all the writing experiences we might face. Revision of persona is much assisted by time; this is another application of the Law of Delay. After some days pass and we can read our own drafts as though they were someone else's, we can see which words create wrong impressions and which words help.

ACTIVITY 11–4: MEMO TO THE BOSS

This activity asks you to establish a very particular persona. Think first about a job you have held or hold and about some minor problem connected to it. Perhaps scheduling, or cooperation among workers, or something about working conditions might come to mind.

Draft a memo to your boss, in which you bring this matter to his or her attention. You could suggest a solution if you have one, but you need not. Your effort should go into trying to sound friendly, polite, concerned, helpful, and of course authoritative.

STYLE SHEETS

Particularly if you become an engineer or a scientist, but also if you go into business, law, medicine, or a wide range of other fields, you will encounter "style sheets" or "style manuals" or "specifications for writing." The word "style" here refers not to meaning and pattern but rather to all the details of laying out sentences on the page—how to document sources, how exactly to punctuate (does that comma go inside or outside the quotation marks?), how to hyphenate and do all the other mechanical things that must be standardized before your writing can be printed and distributed. People are sometimes surprised to find that the standards differ from field to field, but of course the needs of different fields dictate variations and arbitrary points might be decided differently as well.

Even if there aren't official documents on how to write in your field, there are probably strong expectations about how things will be put on paper and what you must do to be correct. Learning these details of style is like learning your manners. Manners differ from place to place and group to group, but within a group the standards are quite distinct. If you want to be read and understood within the group, you will absorb these expectations as rapidly as you can.

Some of the best-known style manuals are those of the American Psychological Association, the Chicago *Tribune*, and the Associated Press. Various branches of the federal government and many state governments also have their own manuals. Other fields might have too few requirements to justify a complete manual, but writers might have to adhere to the rules just as strictly as if a manual existed. Finding out about such a set of rules is a good way to introduce yourself to writing in your field.

ACTIVITY 11–5: USING STYLE MANUALS

The best source of information about standards in your field would be the official style manual. But it might not be easy to find one. Your best bet might be to ask someone already in the field for a copy or a reference to the standards manual.

If you are unable to find such a manual, you might have to use your ingenuity. By looking at publications in the field in the library, for example, you can draw conclusions about the standards you face. You might look to see whether the first-person pronoun is used, whether the passive is used more than the active voice of verbs, how sources are documented in an article, whether articles need subheadings or section titles, and so on. You might also see how examples are presented and at what level of detail.

Write a short "guide to style" in the field you choose. What are the main points a beginner needs to notice?

A FINAL NOTE:
STYLE AND YOUR FUTURE WRITING

The activities of this chapter, like this book as a whole, are meant to help you in your future writing. They show some of the details of how your writing works on readers (the CLOZE activity with your own writing and the letter to a boss), and suggest ways of tailoring your writing to achieve maximum effect on readers (reading word by word, examining style manuals in your field).

But these activities really don't do more than point the way. One area where recent research has shown important gains is clarity; we are beginning to understand how and why keeping to the same subject in a paragraph improves reader comprehension. Another distinct area is the importance of collaboration in writing, finding someone to help you overcome your weak spots and build on your strengths in such matters as word choice and sentence structure. Every writer seems to need this kind of impartial look from someone else, and an important part of your future writing should be finding someone to play this role for you.

This chapter also gives a preview of future writing classes, where you likely will be able to specialize more in the kinds of writing you will do after schooling ends. In those classes, under the label of "style," you will find discussion of the concerns of this chapter.

CHAPTER 12

Revising and Editing

THE POINT OF THIS CHAPTER

The very *last* changes you make in a piece of writing before it goes to its audience are generated within *proofreading*. The term comes from printing, where a "proof" or test copy is made from the metal type before a print run starts. This test copy is used to make minor corrections at the last minute. Obviously, once the type is set, changes are difficult and therefore expensive, so not much is generally done at this point beyond cleaning up punctuation, spelling, and a few other relatively simple problems. By custom, "proof-reading" has continued to mean these small last-minute changes.

The changes immediately *before* proofreading are generally lumped together under the term *editing*. Editing of work about to be published is often done by someone other than the writer because other people can see problems that a writer can't see in how one sentence leads to another, how a paragraph holds together, how the sections of a report fit together, and so forth. Being consistent throughout a long piece of writing is not easy, and if you are the writer you might find it almost impossible, for example, to use a technical term in the same way through ten pages or always to remember what you have assumed an audience knows about your subject. But other people can follow terms and assumptions much more easily because their memories are not clouded by their intentions. They can focus more easily on what you have actually said. If you must edit for yourself, there are many things you can do to make your job easier, but nothing works as well as another mind engaged in the task.

The changes you make before editing are called *revising*. But revising really isn't a separate stage, as we have seen. The things people do when they revise are exactly the things people do when they write. Revision literally means re-seeing, but the ways we re-see are the ways we see. It's just that almost all writing has to be reviewed and changed as it moves from the private world of the writer to the public world of the reader.

One generalization about revising that does stand up pretty well is that it isn't simple. The great myth about revising is that it is after-the-fact repairing of things that have gone wrong. Beginning writers almost always confuse revising with editing or even with proofreading. They put some words on paper, check that the words are spelled correctly and punctuated properly, and think that good writing is writing that is correct.

But revising goes on from the very beginning of the writing process and is essential whether things have gone wrong *or right* in the drafting. Revision is essential because none of us can think about all aspects of a topic at once. Writing a draft can include only some aspects, and the fact that we have written something down means that we can take time to reconsider, add, fill out, develop, prune and weed, to take care of the other aspects that we need to consider. For some writers, revising is the way we get smarter on paper. For others, it might be the way we bring new perspectives to bear. Generally, it is the way we build in considerations of our readers.

In this book, you have already encountered many of the techniques people use for revising. More important than any technique, however, is thinking about revision as an integral part of writing. Once a writer understands how revision helps and why it is necessary, the appropriate techniques will almost suggest themselves. This chapter tries to show why revising is essential and how it helps.

READING AND REVISING

How does revision affect a reader? In unrevised writing, we can generally see traces of how the words were composed.

These traces are especially obvious in rough drafts, where hesitations, rewordings, wanderings, and so forth can be quite distracting to a reader. Even in better-developed drafts, however, we might figure things out as we go and say a point differently after we explain it than we did before. Some added piece of evidence might lead us to rethink a point, even change our minds about it. We might find a colloquial expression the handiest way to express something even though we know that the whole writing is supposed to be more formal.

Even worse, in unrevised writing readers might *not* be able to see the connections that hold an argument together, or show how an example supports a point, or link two sections. The connection can seem perfectly obvious to a writer and yet be completely mysterious to even the sharpest reader. These traces of a writer's composing processes obviously work against a reader.

Most serious of all, in unrevised writing we generally get no sense of significance. Most writers begin with their own concerns, naturally, because these concerns make them want to communicate with readers. But these concerns are narrow, individual, and often expressed in words that give no clear indication of why anyone else should care about them. A major task for revision is then to make significances clear to readers who do not share the point of view of the writer.

By contrast, in revised writing, most traces of the writing process have disappeared. A few may be left, somewhat dressed up, in the path of reasoning that a paper presents. This path of reasoning mimics the reasoning that a person might do; although it is usually far longer and more complex (see Chapter Seven), it might seem effortless. Novice writers are often put off by this appearance of a writing process in the writing; they think that what looks easy and direct must have been composed easily and directly. Experienced writers know otherwise.

A major goal of revision is to accommodate the point of view of the reader. Part of the job of reasoning, as presented in Chapter Six, is to allow the reader to help construct the meaning of a text by finding areas of common ground between reader and writer that can be used as starting points for a discussion. Sometimes this point of view is present from the beginning of the writing process, but, because some generative activities are private, this point of view must sometimes be revised into the writing if it is to be truly accessible to readers.

Another important goal of revision concerns purpose and plan. Chapter Eight displayed the connection between ideas and forms, suggesting that ideas don't come to exist publicly until they have some form or other by which they can be put across to readers. A writer's main idea thus combines a purpose with a structure or organization by the time the writer-reviser has finished looking at form.

ACTIVITY 12–1: RESEEING PERSONAL WRITING

For this activity, choose a journal entry or some of your freewriting that holds together around some topic. The writing should be between fifty and a hundred words long.

Think of this personal writing as a zero draft and prepare a first draft. To start, change every word as you prepare the personal writing for a general audience. You need not use fancy words, but use words that fit a more formal situation. As you do so, you are paraphrasing yourself, of course, and you are paraphrasing in a specific direction—toward a general and unknown reader.

You will also need to add words and sentences to help a reader understand why the topic is interesting, the idea important, the reflection significant. One way of doing this is to place your writing in a larger context: the accident that happened to you that day is part of a pattern of accidents on that road, or an effect of your driving habits, or beyond your control and simply a matter of chance, or perhaps of fate.

WRITING AND REVISING

You can revise in at least as many ways as you initially compose. Good writers don't necessarily have better ideas; instead, they make more of the ideas they do have by their wealth of revising techniques. Many professional writers enjoy telling interviewers how many times they have revised something—ten, fifteen times or more. But effective revision isn't determined only by the number of times you go back through your writing. It's determined by what you do when you go back.

One of the most difficult things for any writer to do is admit that a piece of writing needs help. Facing the fact that the words written down need to be changed is the single biggest obstacle for student writers in particular. We tend to value whatever is in print—especially if we have labored to put it down—and to think that "what's done is done."

But what's done is never really done because, as we have seen, there is no one best way of saying anything. For every well-chosen word, there is an audience who won't be affected but who could be reached by some other word. The meaning of what you write isn't fixed, either, and so, as you revise, the meaning is always growing, changing direction, abandoning some ground and gaining other ground elsewhere. Mostly, our revision comes to a stop against a deadline; at some point, we say, "Enough—now I really must move to editing and polishing."

ACTIVITY 12–2: REVISING AFTER PUBLICATION

The essayist and novelist Gore Vidal revises his novels after they have been published. He is partly joking—he is making it difficult for literary critics to decide which version of the novel is the one that really represents his thinking the best. But he is partly serious, too; at least one of his books has been reissued after the revision.

You too can revise something after it has been published. Choose some newspaper article that interests you from last week's newspaper or from a news magazine. Now that the event isn't news (or now that you know about further developments), revise a short section of eight or ten sentences from the article as it might appear now (perhaps it will be background for some future event). You almost inevitably shorten when you do this, and you will make other changes, too, depending on the content of your article.

Once you have understood that *all* writing can be usefully revised, you can begin thinking about the ways in which you should revise your own work. For many people, the hardest part of this thinking is letting go of the words written down first. There is no way around it. Something must be sacrificed to the improvements you want to make even if you save the words to use again some other time.

ACTIVITY 12–3: LETTING GO

This activity consists simply of throwing away a piece of writing. It can be a piece of freewriting, a journal entry, a finished essay from last term, whatever you like. But it must be irretrievably thrown away. Make it impossible for yourself to have second thoughts.

If you have ever had a computer "lose" some of your writing, you know the sudden empty feeling that is the point of this activity. Nothing is quite as gone as the order among a group of electrons, erased by a single keystroke or a power failure and vanished into the electricity.

The important part of this activity is reflection. Why should such a loss be difficult? After all, if we thought something out before, we can think it out again, right? And we can probably remember approximately what we were saying.

My own thoughts abut the loss required by the previous activity are that we entrust to the page or screen words that we are not planning on remembering. We give the words attention as we write them, and that attention is directed outward to the words, not inward to them. We make objects of them, give them a life outside ourselves, even if all we are doing is freewriting. And we value these traces of our thought. External as they are, they show us to ourselves. They take on an order or plan that we cannot hold in our heads easily, since we can rarely attend to many thoughts at once while the page can hold many simultaneously.

There are probably many other reasons, and some individual ones too, that make throwing away a piece of writing difficult for most of us. Whatever the causes you decide on to explain your feelings about this matter, you will almost surely recognize what writers often say, that this feeling of loss is the other side of the coin in revising.

We want to revise (or we learn to) because we care about our writing in the ways we can identify when we lose some. Even if the writing is merely to satisfy an arbitrary assignment, the words we choose are still a reflection of our position in regard to that assignment and represent an investment of time and effort. Once we have written, we have a new possession. We are also possessed in a way by the words, since they reveal something of ourselves and our abilities.

But the motivation to revise is crucial to succeeding as a writer. We have somehow to recognize, in the sacrifices of words we have written, the attraction that writing can have for us, whether it is the potential it carries for us to know and expand our own minds, the chance to make our own views newly powerful and capable of reaching others, or the opportunity to gain clarity in thinking through the organizing power of structures. Writing begins to function for us when we arrive at precisely the motivation that will lead us to revise.

REASONING AND REVISING

Reasoning as presented in Chapter Six is changing a view or opinion or idea in light of some new thought or experience or evidence or in light of a new perspective. As a reasoner, I change my thoughts or words when I see that I can fit together things that were unrelated, when for instance I see how one event causes another and helps me predict it. Perhaps I come to see how the pattern of a particular experience I have had is similar to another. Perhaps I realize I have been inconsistent, treating myself in one way and other people in another way, and on reflection I decide I should treat myself and others the same, gaining more of what is called "coherence" in my beliefs and actions by doing so. These kinds of changes are characteristic of the reasoning we do every day. "Aha, *now* I see," we say as we near the end of some reasoning.

Reasoning of this kind *is* revising. Revising is literally re-seeing or re-viewing, getting a new view of things. How can you gain such a new view?

As so often in writing, the first step is the hardest; here the first step is in simply reflecting on what you have already written. Reflecting doesn't mean thinking the same thoughts again, the way a pond reflects the trees around it. Reflecting in our minds means wondering whether something is true, wondering if we could be wrong, wondering if we have enough evidence, raising questions and objections, trying to see past our prejudices, stereotypes, automatic opinions, taking away the authority of the version we have just written. No trick can perform this step for us. It might be that only maturity can do it, that the only way we can revise is by accepting some uncertainties. It might even be that this quality above all separates adolescents from adults—the tolerance for uncertainty.

Once you have reached a new view about the writing you are revising, it is usually not hard to recognize the pattern of your thinking. All these lines of thought or revising work by making genuine and attractive alternatives to the version of things already written out, not so much by flatly contradicting it as by modifying it in some realistic and useful way. We have already seen that simply waiting will often help give a new perspective on our writing, as we forget precisely what we intended and begin to be able to see what we have said (the Law of Delay). Some of the other ways people have arrived at successful revision include:

1. Explaining the point to someone not in the original audience (for example, rephrasing as if writing a personal letter or answering the implied challenge, "Come on now, what does that really amount to?")

2. Simply developing a new example of the point that shows its limits, assumptions, gaps, and so on

3. Paraphrasing ("What I *really* meant to say was . . .")

4. Changing the "mode" or method—changing from problem-and-solution, perhaps, to cause-and-effect, or definition, or classification, or analysis, or comparison, and so on

5. Restructuring, such as by outlining and assigning each section of the outline a specific function ("Introduce the topic through a story" and so on)

6. Drawing some large generalization from the writing already done, setting that material in a broader context to see what it amounts to

7. Imagining that someone you hate has just presented your position and finding some way in which the person doesn't yet understand the full story, all the complexity, the real underlying truth

8. Writing a before-and-after ("I used to think [the first draft], but now I think . . .")

9. Thoroughly rewording the whole piece, for instance, by putting it into more or less formal words

10. Explaining why the topic is hard (or easy)

These are all reflections after the fact, which means that they are not necessarily what the reviser was thinking about during the revision. One does not always know where the new view comes from, but the specific strategy is less important than making the possibility of an alternative view a *real* possibility.

ACTIVITY 12–4: REFLECTING

Carefully read a piece of writing you would like to revise and then put it out of sight. Freewrite as rapidly as you can for five minutes about the writing.

To help you get started, you might quickly read these questions, using any that help.

What seems to push the writing or hold it back?
What would give it extra zip?
What would it look like inside out or backwards?
What would an alien think of it?
What parts of it feel right?
Who would read it in a movie, and how?
What color is it?
Where is its weak point?
Who could doubt it and why?

It is in revising that the real connections between writing and learning become most tangible. Learning doesn't occur in a vacuum, and it isn't the filling of an empty container. It is instead the expansion or development of things that are already known. Begun by reflection, questioning, and doubt, learning can simply mean that we reinforce existing beliefs in new ways. Or it can mean that we satisfy curiosity, fill a gap with needed information or a desirable skill, arrive at a destination we already had clearly in view. Or yet again it can mean that we become wiser, change from a simple view to a more adequate complex one, advance beyond the familiar and the already given and the automatic to a fresh and more accurate understanding. Finally it can mean an actual loss, as we give up some secure certainty in favor of a more reasonable doubt. These are all possible, and valuable, outcomes of the kind of learning we label revision.

ACTIVITY 12–5: REVISING

Once you know that revising can be done in many ways, you can translate this know-that into know-how. Choose some writing that you want to revise and consciously choose some way of going about the revision.

When you have reached the end of your revision process, make copies of the before-and-after versions for your writing group and explain what you have done. What kind of reviser were you on this occasion? What suggestions do they have for alternative methods that you might like?

EDITING

Revising isn't necessarily distinct from writing itself, we have said, and similarly it isn't necessarily distinct from editing either, if by editing we mean the methods of getting a text ready for readers. A typical editing change such as removing the first paragraph—we all tend to start a little slowly, and often we can do without the first hesitant steps—can have dramatic effects on how we think about our topic, and so it can be considered a form of revising. Sometimes that first paragraph can be usefully moved to the end of the writing, where it functions as a kind of summary; here again what we might see ourselves doing is reversing the order in which we think about our topic. If you are more comfortable keeping the "stages" of revising and editing combined, you should do so.

If you keep the two kinds of activity distinct, however, one question you might save for editing is that of size. The length you assign to your different ideas, for example, tells readers how important each one is in comparison with the others. In editing, you might decide to change this comparison, expanding some ideas that seem to need greater prominence and reducing others that are less central to your view.

ACTIVITY 12–6: EXPANDING AND CONTRACTING

From an already revised piece of writing, choose a paragraph that seems to need either drastic expansion or drastic compression. Double or halve the length, as you think appropriate.

These changes in size should not feel like padding or sacrificing. Expanding a paragraph into two, for example, might mean finding additional examples, generating fifty more specifics about the topic, moving more slowly through the connections between two ideas, or showing more clearly why two ideas are *not* connected. Compressing may mean finding a word to stand in for a phrase, finding parallel sentence structures for similar ideas and eliminating repetition, or combining sentences.

Good editors also look for a multitude of other ways to improve prose. They clarify structure, adjust paragraphing, improve transitions, and so on. Editing is also a profession, as you would expect of such an advanced set of skills. These are some of the matters you can expect to work on in later writing courses.

PROOFREADING

Correctness matters. The chapter on grammar (Chapter Ten) suggests ways you can increase your knowledge of the forms of English. The task of this section is somewhat different because the problems of a writer are both short and long term. Increasing your knowledge of English is a long-term project, but fixing the problems in a piece of writing today—proofreading—are short term. The problem in the short term is, first, learning to spot errors and, second, learning what to do about them.

I recommend that you begin keeping a record of the kinds of problems you have. You might have trouble spelling certain words or kinds of words (for example, is it -*ent* or -*ant*?). You might characteristically miss sentence boundaries and commit comma splices or fragments. Improvement results first from keeping track. But this is still rather a long-term strategy if your problem is to get a particular paper in shape.

Unlike revising and editing, proofreading can be improved by some tricks. These have the common aim of helping you look at your work as if it were someone else's, because it is much easier to spot errors this way.

One of the simplest techniques for proofreading is to read the paper aloud to yourself. If this does not give you enough "distance" on your writing, one of the suggestions in the next activity might.

ACTIVITY 12–7: PROOFREADING—SEEING THE INVISIBLE

All these techniques have the aim of making your writing seem strange to you. If you are working alone, read your revised and edited piece backwards, one sentence at a time. Or read it aloud into a tape recorder, and then read along as that strange voice performs your words. Or read it in a strange accent, John Wayne, or Pee Wee Herman, or someone from another country. Watch for subjects and their predicates, or other features you know have been a problem for you in the past.

A FINAL NOTE: THE PAIN AND GAIN OF WRITING

Getting your writing ready for its audience means growing beyond your usual boundaries. You have to see your writing as someone else would. That means you have to identify specific traits of someone else and adopt them temporarily (much as you might project yourself into the main character of a novel). Writers grow in this way, and that growth is one of the reasons people find writing worthwhile despite the difficulties of doing it well.

CHAPTER 13

Learning to Write All Over Again

THE POINT OF THIS CHAPTER

To many people, writing seems like a skill that is separate from the writer and pretty much the same for everyone. Sometimes it seems like the same skill in different situations or at different times. But we know from the nature of reading, as well as from the nature of writing and revising, that these appearances are misleading.

What is writing, really? And what does it take to learn it? How should we think about writing in order to be prepared to meet the writing tasks we will face in the future?

WRITING FOR THE FUTURE

Writing is a great deal more than a skill. It contains a number of skills within it, to be sure, but its nature is different. The essence or core of writing is change.

It changes with the situation and with the person. In an essay test, a writer might write one way, while with more time to think, the same writer might write a different way. Different writers respond quite differently to the essay test or the more leisurely situation, and rightly so. This changing nature of writing, its plasticity, comes from the changing nature of its possible audiences, from the different things readers do with words, and from the nature of the efforts writers can make to lead readers in one direction or another. Writers seek to begin in common territory, with ideas to which they expect agreement from readers, and these areas change with the audience. Writers seek to find means of convincing readers, and these means will also change with audience. Writers seek to find ways to present themselves effectively, and these ways will change not only with different audiences but also with different selves, with the different partial personalities summoned to the writing task in different situations. Writers seek ways of revising their writing into reasonable material, trying to think as audiences think—and there is no end to the process of adjusting to audiences.

The plasticity of writing—coming from the changing nature of the audience, of ideas, and of the writer's self—means that writing cannot be learned once and for all. The similarities among different kinds of writing are not great enough to allow them to transfer perfectly from one to the next as we often mistakenly assume. When any writer meets a new set of requirements, that writer will question his or her writing process, the areas of agreement with the audience, the needs of the audience for new material, the kind of structure that the material and the audience seem to suggest, and so on.

Professional writers know all this; perhaps what makes a professional writer of almost any kind—technical writer or advertising writer or science writer or journalist or essayist or other— what makes any of us into a person who writes comfortably along with our other activities is this willingness to live with uncertainty, to start all over again, to rethink from the ground up. What all of us can do, professional or not, is prepare to change our writing by developing a flexible attitude and experimenting with a wide repertoire of activities so that we can choose and develop the new kind of writing we need today *and* the one we need tomorrow.

We as writers might think we are deficient when the new situation or audience makes us feel "rusty." The truth is that, because of the new situation, we are seeing freshly the difficulties built into the nature of writing.

How does a writer adapt best? This book has argued that we as writers need first to learn how to learn, so that we can examine each new situation carefully and confidently. The second step is to learn broader and more flexible ways of reading than those that are generally taught so that we can put ourselves into our readers' places more easily and anticipate the many things that readers can legitimately do when reading our words. A competent writer then adapts to readers, drawing on a repertoire of writing processes for just the right techniques to get started, to structure, to revise—in short, a competent writer is a flexible writer. The essence of this competence is the willingness to rethink. A competent writer extends the idea of revision from the page to the activity itself.

In other words, a good writer is one who learns to write all over again in each new situation. The consequences of this idea might at first seem disappointing—you mean there isn't any end to this learning?—but they are in fact the consequences of a view of education, of learning, and of knowledge that are becoming quite widespread as people try to adapt to a world of change in all fields of study and in all walks of life. Life is more interesting this way, more fun, more challenging.

The real activity or exercise for this chapter will not come inside this book. It will not come inside the writing course you are now taking. It will come the week after the course is over, or the month after, or ten years after. This book tries to reach into the future, but it can go only so far because, of course, too much of the future is unknown. The content you will need you must supply yourself; what this book has tried to supply are the materials and some indications of the attitudes we must have if we are to grow and develop as writers. This book can't be finished, can't conclude. It can only try to open outward, and it can encourage you to do the same.

ACTIVITY 13–1: A SMALL STEP

For this activity, you should write something fairly small and make a small change in the way you ordinarily write.

The content should come from something you have been thinking about, something that seems to want you to write about it, and the audience should be perhaps just a little different from the audience you usually write for. Most important, you should deliberately alter the way you write it, using a technique or strategy you haven't used before.

Perhaps you usually compose with a pencil and this time decide to try writing your first draft at a typewriter or using a microcomputer. Perhaps you usually try to get the first draft perfect and decide this time to revise completely. Perhaps you usually write all by yourself and decide this time to get some response from someone early in your writing process.

Whatever change you make, it should feel risky, a bit dangerous or frightening or uncomfortable. "I don't belong here, I'm not really allowed to do this, I have no right to think I can do this, or I might take some heat for this." You might want to think of this writing as a pure experiment—"I'm doing this just to see what happens if I . . ." Or you might use this opportunity to write in a way you think you'll never use, in a drama, a poem, or a story. What you are doing, in effect, is finding one of your boundaries and deliberately crossing it.

The most important part of this writing is not what someone else thinks of it. Instead, its value is your evaluation of it. You need not decide it is great writing to get the most out of the attempt. Instead, you should try to see how the boundary-crossing looks and feels to you. Only you know whether you were able to face the requirement that you experiment, deliberately vary the activities you have already mastered, and go beyond safe territory.

INDEX